LIFE IN
TUDOR ENGLAND

An early Tudor nobleman: the image of virility

Life in
TUDOR
ENGLAND

PENRY WILLIAMS

English Life Series
Edited by PETER QUENNELL

LONDON: B. T. BATSFORD LTD
NEW YORK: G. P. PUTNAM'S SONS

To My Mother

First published 1964

© Penry Williams, 1964

Made and printed in Great Britain
by William Clowes and Sons, Limited, London and Beccles
for the publishers
B. T. BATSFORD LTD
4 Fitzhardinge Street, Portman Square, London, W.1
G. P. PUTNAM'S SONS
200 Madison Avenue, New York 16, N.Y.

Preface

A page of explanation is needed on the scope of this book. It takes its place in this series between Mr Bagley's *Life in Medieval England* and Professor Dodd's *Life in Elizabethan England*, and it has been designed to show how the England of the Yorkists was transformed into the England of Elizabeth. The critical period for understanding that change is, I think, the half-century from 1520 to 1570 and it is upon this period that I have focussed attention. But there are no firm dates in social history and I have not hesitated to range far back into the fifteenth century or well forward to the end of the sixteenth.

The central period with which this book deals was, in England, barren of good painting and drawing. The great English tradition of illuminated manuscripts had died by the middle of the fifteenth century; miniatures and engravings were not produced in any great number until the reign of Elizabeth. It has not therefore been easy to choose adequate contemporary illustrations. But while I have often had to go outside the strict limits of my period for a picture, and have occasionally had to go outside England, I am confident that the pictures chosen illustrate the life of the sixteenth century, even if some of them were executed at a later date. However, what the early Tudor period lacks in pictures it gains in words. The outspoken, virile language of the time conveys a firm and vivid impression of men's thoughts and lives; I have quoted from it as often as I could.

As to my own prose, I am grateful to my wife for the skill and patience with which she has eliminated its worst infelicities: those that remain are my fault alone.

February 1964   P. W.

Contents

Acknowledgment

The frontispiece and the illustration on page 163 are reproduced by gracious permission of Her Majesty The Queen. The Author and the Publishers wish to thank the following for the illustrations appearing in this book: the Warden and Fellows of All Souls College, Oxford for page 39; Hallam Ashley, F.R.P.S. for page 90 (bottom); the Ashmolean Museum, Oxford for page 78; John Aubrey-Fletcher and the Buckinghamshire Record Office for page 32; the Court of the Worshipful Company of Barbers for page 108; Public Art Collection, Basle for page 71; the Marquess of Bath for page 82; Staatliche Museen, Berlin for page 56; the Trustees of the British Museum for pages 4, 5, 6, 7, 8, 12, 17, 20–1, 33, 35, 36 (both), 40 (left), 45, 50, 62, 66, 68, 72, 76, 93, 95, 97, 98, 99 (both), 103, 104, 106, 111 (both), 112, 115, 119, 121, 123, 137, 141, 145, 150, 162, 166–7 and 169; Cambridge University Library for page 37; Dawsons of Pall Mall for pages 109 and 110; the Rt. Hon. Viscount De L'Isle, V.C. (from his Collection at Penshurst Place, Kent) for page 122; the Essex Record Office for pages 51, 52 and 105; the Trustees of the Goodwood Collection (and Longmans, Green & Co. Ltd.) for page 58; A. F. Kersting, F.R.P.S. for page 86; the London Museum for pages 18 (bottom) and 19 (top); the Director of the National Maritime Museum, Greenwich for page 75; the National Portrait Gallery for pages 46, 47, 48, 54, 74, 142, 143 and 167; the Warden and Fellows of New College, Oxford for pages 130 and 131; the Mansell Collection for pages 84, 85 and 91; the *Radio Times* Hulton Picture Library for pages 83 (bottom), 87, 88, 92, 140 and 154; Dr J. K. St Joseph for page 40 (right); the Trustees of the Victoria and Albert Museum for page 118.

The jacket illustration of the London Merchant Georg Gisze, by Hans Holbein (1532), is reproduced by courtesy of Preussischer Kulturbesitz Staatliche Museen, Gëmaldegalerie, Berlin Dahlem.

viii

The Illustrations

I

The Land

About the time of the dissolution of the monasteries a sad-looking man with hooked nose and drooping mouth began to explore the counties of England and Wales. For eight years he travelled from town to town, riding over the countryside, noting down its villages, bridges, parks, mansions, and antiquities, anything indeed that caught his interest. This man was the Reverend John Leland, father of the long line of topographers and historians who have educated generations in the English scene. He was the Pevsner of his day.

'Inflamed', as he told Henry VIII, 'inflamed with a love to see thoroughly all those parts of this your opulent and ample realm', determined that 'the old glory of your renowned Britain . . . flourish through the world', he travelled the coast and the interior, 'sparing neither labour nor costs' until he had seen all that was to be seen. Then he set himself to write. But before he had finished his work, Leland, 'by a most pitiful occasion fell beside his wits'. Of his intended monument to the greatness of Britain there remain eight manuscript volumes, some of them soon allowed to become 'moth-eaten, mouldy, and rotten', all of them full of disjointed and fascinating material.

Leland's achievement seems all the greater when one considers the difficulty of travel. Instead of the national road system that we know today, there was merely a hopeful injunction that each parish should maintain its own highways. It is not surprising that the roads in general were 'very

The fortified bridge at Monmouth

noisome and tedious to travel in', that a 'foul and noyful slough' was reported on the Chelmsford-Stock road, or that a street in Thaxted was said to be 'so gulled with the fall of the water that passengers cannot pass'. Crossing rivers was a more complicated business still, for bridges strong enough to withstand flood waters were costly to build and a bridge was consequently something of a rarity and an occasion. Most of them carried a cross and some even carried chapels; others, like Monmouth Bridge, were built with a small fortress above them; and they were all unusual enough for Leland to note down carefully those that he crossed. Often rivers had to be forded, which could be a difficult matter, as he found on his way from Clyro to Hay-on-Wye: 'after passing over Wye River, the which for lack of good knowledge in me of the ford, did sore trouble my horse, I came *in crepusculo* to the Hay.'

Leland travelled on horseback, like almost everyone else of his day, for wheeled vehicles were not much used for passengers. Although the Middle Ages had known so-called 'chariots or whirlicotes', they were only for noblewomen or princes and must have been unbearably bone-shaking on early Tudor roads. Only in the middle of the sixteenth century were coaches brought to England, and even then they seem to have been confined to London, where they quickly brought about the traffic problem that has been growing ever since. On horseback a man could move surprisingly fast: the 170 miles from London to Exeter took only three days. News travelled faster still by the royal couriers, who, by changing horses, could carry a

letter from Plymouth to
London in two days and
from Dover to London in
24 hours. But this service
was only open to a few.

By following John
Leland on his travels
through England and by
filling out his descriptions
with the comments of
other writers, we can

Queen Elizabeth's coach

see the land as it appeared to a contemporary. In this brief
tour of the realm we shall first move north up the eastern
midlands to the Scottish border, then south through Wales
and its Marches to Cornwall, and finally eastwards to the
Home Counties and London. Although we shall not have
space to mention more than a small sample of counties,
we shall obtain a reliable impression of the country as
a whole.

We come first to Leicestershire, lying in the heart of England
and typical of the midland counties. It was hard country for a
journey, and even at the end of the next century Daniel Defoe
complained that on reaching the midlands, 'you enter the deep
clays, which are so surprisingly soft, that it is perfectly frightful
to travellers'. Leland seems, however, to have found it pleasant
enough. The countryside was 'plentiful of corn and pasture',
with 'exceeding fair and large meadows' on both sides of the
River Welland; for this was essentially a region of mixed
farming, with soil suitable for crops or for grazing. Very few
woods were to be seen and most of the farming was still
conducted in the medieval open-field system. It was a county of
rich, independent peasants, and in some of its villages there
was no squire or manor-house. Leland, however, was not much
interested in peasants and has nothing to say about them. He
reserves his comments for the great families, telling us, for
instance, that the Greys of Groby had begun a 'great gate
house of brick and a tower' and had made a 'fair park' at
Bradgate. Indeed his account of England, like Saxton's maps

John Leland (1506–52)

50 years later, is well sprinkled with mentions of the parks of the aristocracy.

Leicester itself, the largest borough in the shire, was a small market town of about 3,000 inhabitants, largely dependent upon the surrounding countryside for the meat, milk, and leather traded by its burgesses. Once, it had known rather grander days when the dukes of Lancaster had lived in Leicester Castle, but by Leland's time the castle was disused and was dismissed by him as 'a thing of small estimation'. The houses, all 'builded of timber', were mostly small and cramped. In short, the town was not very impressive and probably fitted already the description of it by John Evelyn: an 'old and ragged city . . . large and pleasantly seated, but despicably built'.

The next county, Lincolnshire, was a strange mixture. In the south it was open-field country, 'fertile of corn and grass', not much different from Leicestershire. There were three long fingers of upland, mostly of poor, thin soil where sheep were bred for wool. To the east lay the Fenland, which Leland, like most other travellers, avoided. The fen country around the Wash long gave Lincolnshire a bad reputation. Henry VIII spoke of it as one of the 'most brute and beastly' shires of his realm. A schoolmaster, having spent two years at Crowland, found the climate 'so unwholesome, that he would rather die than pass a third summer there'. In the next century Samuel Pepys spoke of travelling over 'most sad fens, all the way observing the sad life which the people of the place do live'. To the outsider that life seemed to be mostly fishing and wild-fowling. In Michael Drayton's words,

The toiling fisher here is towing of his net;
The fowler is employed, his limed twigs to set.

4

But it was not always like this. Fishing and fowling were winter pursuits, followed when much of the fenland was under water. In summer the livestock could be brought out from their refuges on to pastures left by the retreating floods. The country, in the words of its defenders, was no 'mere quagmire', but the breeding-ground of 'infinite number of serviceable horses, mares and colts', 'great store of young cattle', and 'great flocks of sheep'. But few outsiders penetrated it and few of the upper classes cared to live there. 'The want of gentlemen here to inhabit' worried a government look-

An angler

ing for potential justices of the peace; but it was not much lamented by the peasants, who, until the draining of the fens, were happily free from the deer-parks and enclosures of the squires.

The city of Lincoln had been one of the richest and most impressive towns of medieval England. But when Leland reached it there were signs of poverty and decline. He was shocked to see one parish church 'in clear ruin' and to find that only 23 others survived, out of an original 38. Since the mayor and corporation were busily pulling down disused churches in order to use the stone for repairing walls, pavements, dykes, and other churches, this disappearance is not very surprising. Nor were churches the only buildings to come down, for many private houses were dilapidated or deserted. All this was sign of what the town council itself called 'the great and "unrecup-able" decay of the city', brought about by the departure elsewhere of much of Lincoln's wool trade.

England north of the River Trent has traditionally been thought barbarous, remote, and poor. Nothing could be less true of Yorkshire. Leland is full of phrases like 'meetly good corn ground', 'pasture and meadow and some woods'. The

Scarborough, a decayed sea-port

aristocracy and gentry had made their mark with castles, houses, and parks—like the 'very pretty house' built by Mr Lascelles at Brackenborough. There were noble towns: some, like Hull, 'waxed very rich'; others, like Scarborough, where the pier was 'now sore decayed', had passed their best. The greatest of all, York, though poorer than it had been, was still a provincial capital.

It is not until one reaches the border shires—Northumberland, Cumberland, Westmorland—that the north presents a bleaker and more primitive face. Here, in the words of William Camden, an Elizabethan topographer, were 'barren places, which cannot easily by the painful labour of the husbandman be brought to fruitfulness'. This was a country of violence and vendetta, where, at the head of beautiful, unwelcoming dales, lived marauding border clans. These moss-troopers lived on plunder, raiding the farms north and south of the border and following the feud among themselves—'deadly feud, the word of enmity in the borders, implacable without the blood and whole family destroyed'. Leland saw the signs of ruin all about him. Family after family had come to poverty through lawlessness: the 'Davells' lands were attainted and sparkled' by Edward II, so that there now remained only 'mean gentlemen of the name'; one of the Rudhams had 'killed a man of name', and lost thereby £600 a year, causing his descendant to be 'but a man of mean lands'.

Against the violence of the moss-troopers and the Scots beyond the border, houses had to be strong. Great nobles built castles like Alnwick and Naworth. The gentry built pele-towers, which were fortified houses on three storeys—the lowest for stores, the first floor for the hall, the second floor for sleeping, and the roof for fighting. The moss-troopers built timber cabins, whose outer walls were 'made of great . . . oak trees strongly bound and joined together with great "tenons" of the same'.

In all these border counties Leland saw only one thing that brought out his praise. Of Newcastle-on-Tyne he wrote that 'the strength and magnificence of the walling of this town far passeth all the walls of the cities of England and of most of the towns of Europa'. For us the interest of the town lies less in its walls than in its coal. For here, in backward and undeveloped Northumberland, was one of the most dynamic towns in England. Its merchants had already secured the monopoly of the coal-trade on the Tyne; they were soon to acquire coalfields of their own from the bishop of Durham and to found landed dynasties on the profits of the great mining boom.

Newcastle-on-Tyne, with its magnificent walling

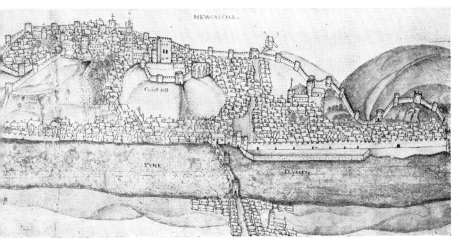

Coming south into the Welsh Marches, we reach Shropshire. Here was a well-wooded country of small farms, averaging 20 acres each, given over mostly to dairying. Its towns had long been engaged in the clothing industry, but several of them, like Lincoln, were now in a bad way. Of Bridgnorth Leland said: 'the town standeth by clothing, and that now decayed there, the town sorely decayeth therewith'. In those days Bridgnorth looked quite different from the spacious, almost Italianate, hill-town of today. Leland said of its main street that on each side 'the houses be galleried, so that men may pass dry by them if it rain, according to [i.e. like] some streets in Chester city'.

Just as London came to stand head and shoulders above all other cities in England, so some country towns were pushing up above their neighbours. Such a town was Shrewsbury. Surrounded on three sides by the Severn—on which the famous Shrewsbury swans were already to be seen—the town defended its fourth side with the strong, sandstone castle which now guards the approach from the railway station. Over the Severn were two bridges: the easterly, the English bridge, was lightly

Shrewsbury and its swans

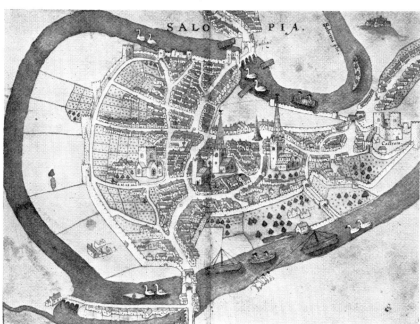

defended; the other, the Welsh bridge, was far more impressive, with a gate at the town end and, at the far side, facing Wales, 'a mighty strong tower to prohibit enemies to enter onto the bridge'. Shrewsbury was, even at this late date, conscious of its role as a frontier town, defending England against the barbarian Welsh. In the words of one of its citizens, it had been and still was 'the greatest strength and defence that His [the King's] subjects of that shire have against the wildness of Wales and Marches'. For the cattle thieves still came down from the hills when the days began to shorten in November. 'Who was he', rhetorically asked an Elizabethan

The Welsh Bridge at Shrewsbury

lawyer, 'who was he of the English counties that bordered upon the skirts of the mountains of Montgomery, Radnor, Brecknock, or Monmouth, that in towns nightly kept not their cattle in folds, and the fear of the mountain thieves caused it?' Shrewsbury then still had its part to play as a marcher town and was careful to make a good show of it; we find the authorities paying a labourer 5d. for 'fixing and putting the head of a certain felon and rebel . . . called Griffith ap Jevan ap David . . . upon a post over the town gate towards Wales to the terror and example of other the like felons and rebels'.

But this frontier role was slowly giving way to another. Shrewsbury's cloth merchants, organised in the Drapers' Company, had achieved a monopoly in buying Welsh-made cloth for the London market, and from the profits of this lucrative trade in cheap and shoddy fabric were built the towering three-storey, half-timbered houses that we can still see today—those that have not been pulled down to make way for banks and

A merchant's house at Shrewsbury

garages. Far from keeping the Welsh out of England, Shrewsbury was attracting them in large numbers with its offers of work and its prospect of riches. The town formed the first step on the emigrant's road to English ways. 'You will find', said an indignant Welshman, 'some men that, so soon as they see the River Severn or the steeples of Shrewsbury, and hear the Englishman but once say good morrow, they shall begin to put their Welsh out of mind and to speak it in most corrupt fashion'.

Leland did not find Wales or the Welsh much to his taste. He remarked sourly of the Cardiganshire hills, that the ground 'is horrible with the sight of bare stones'. Seeing that corn was little grown in much of the country, he observed disapprovingly that 'the Welshmen in times past, as they do almost yet, did study more to pasturage than tilling, as favourers of their consuete [i.e. accustomed] idleness'. Wales was, as a great deal of it is now, a poor country. There were few towns to give it economic drive or to provide a market for the farmer's produce. Most of the towns that there were got a contemptuous report from Leland: Llandovery, for instance, 'a poor market . . . hath but one street and that poorly builded of thatched houses'. But there were one or two that responded vigorously to social changes. At Denbigh, for instance, the old walled town, 'standing somewhat high and on rocky ground', had 'decayed within'. But, next to it, a new town had been built, 'three times as big as the old', in which 'the confluence to the market on Tuesday is exceeding great'.

But in general Wales, a country of poor soil, scattered farms, and tiny hamlets, had little to offer the man ambitious for riches. Certainly the Welsh gentry were poorer than their neighbours across the border. Rowland Lee, president of the Council in the Marches of Wales, wrote of them: 'there be very Welshmen in Wales above Brecknock that may dispend ten pound land, and, to say truth, their discretion less than their lands'. It is not surprising that the sons of gentry and peasants alike should have gone to England to look for fortunes. But those who stayed had, however poor and indiscreet they might be, a fierce and imaginative pride in race and ancestry. A gentleman from Presteign, convinced that his son should be christened in something more aristocratic than water, 'upon a proud stomach caused the water to be voided out of the font and filled it with wine'. It was this sort of pride that made the Welsh gentleman a stock figure of fun in England. But the pride had its deeper and more serious side, which found an outlet in the scholarly concern of some of the best Welsh squires for the history, literature and language of their race. Sir Edward Stradling of Glamorgan for example, built up a fine library at St Donat's, wrote *The Winning of the Lordship of Glamorgan*, and subsidised the publication of a Welsh Grammar.

From one Celtic region to another—Cornwall. Some of this county, Leland noted with approval, was 'fertile of corn and grass', but much of it was 'moorish and hilly ground', with high mountains and rocky soil. Especially in the north, there were very few woods, 'to the which the bleak northern sea is not there of nature favourable'. Nevertheless Leland found a great deal to catch his imagination. Tintagel Castle, he wrote, 'hath been a marvellous strong and notable fortress, and almost *situ loci* inexpugnable, especially for the dungeon that is on a great and high terrible crag, environed with the sea'. There were too some fine churches: Bodmin church, said Leland, is a 'fair large thing'. For in spite of its poor soil Tudor Cornwall, unlike Tudor Wales, was rich. The ground, said Leland,

11

Penzance and the Cornish coast

'barren of his self, yet is fertile by yielding of tin'. All over the country he noted the tin-works which brought wealth to so many—though not to the tin-miners themselves. Feared by Thomas Cely as 'ten thousand or twelve thousand of the roughest and most mutinous men in England', they were in fact a sad race, living apart from other men, working at some risk in a hot and smoky atmosphere. Happier places than the tin-works were the fishing ports, which delighted Leland's eye. Fowey and Falmouth in particular had active harbours, full of fishing vessels and traders. 'Falmouth', said Leland, 'is a haven very notable and famous', for the channel was two miles long and fourteen fathoms deep. At Fowey he was struck less by the harbour than by the men, who, having got rich by war and piracy, 'fell all to merchandise' so that 'the town was haunted with ships of divers nations, and their ships went to all nations'.

Except for his remarks about the men of Fowey, Leland has little to say about the Cornish themselves. They were, however, an interesting and distinctive race, still jealous of their independence. John Norden,

12

writing later in the century, said that they seemed 'yet to retain a kind of concealed envy against the English'. In the west at least they also retained their own tongue, for, Norden says, 'husband and wife, parents and children, master and servants do mutually communicate in their native language'. But most of them could speak English, 'unless it be some obscure people that seldom confer with the better sort'. One can see at work the social pressures that killed Cornish then, as they sapped Welsh later, by representing English as the language of the better sort.

Coming eastwards from Cornwall we reach Wiltshire, a county with a surprisingly specialised economy. In the north was the Cheese Country, mostly devoted to dairying, while to the south lay the Chalk Country, high uplands bearing sheep and corn. But the feature of the county that struck Leland was its cloth manufacture. In Salisbury there was an old textile industry, whose history already stretched back several centuries, while in the west of the county, stretching from Malmesbury to Warminster, there was a new and developing industrial area. Leland remarked that Trowbridge 'flourisheth by drapery' and that 'all the town of Bradford [-on-Avon] standeth by cloth-making'. In Malmesbury he described how the great clothier, William Stumpe, had set up a small factory of looms in the dissolved abbey. But by concentrating upon the towns he gives a slightly misleading picture of the industry. For weaving in this region was a rural occupation, directed by the clothiers in the small towns, actually undertaken by villagers. Almost a century before Leland's day, an earlier antiquarian, William of Worcester, surveyed for his master the manor of Castle Combe. It contained, he said, two hamlets, one called Overcombe, 'where are the husbandmen occupied in cultivating and working the land situated on the high ground', the other called Nethercombe, in the valley-bottom, 'where live the men who are used to make cloth, the weavers, fullers, dyers, and other craftsmen'. His description illustrates very well the village industry of Tudor Wiltshire, with its intermingling of agrarian and industrial pursuits.

'Kent', said Leland, 'is the key of all England'. Its 'commodities' were legion: 'fertility, wood, pasture, cattle, fish, fowl, rivers, havens with ships among the five ports most famous, and royal castles and towns'. Even in Leland's day its soil was prosperous. By the next generation Kent's greatest historian, William Lambarde, was writing with succulent enthusiasm of the fresh fruit supplied to London: 'as for orchards of apples, and gardens of cherries, and those of the most delicious and exquisite kinds that can be, no part of the realm (that I know) hath them'. According to Lambarde, the worth of the people matched the worth of the soil, for the gentlemen were responsible and well-read, the yeomen 'civil, just and bountiful'. But perhaps he was biased.

While the great metropolis of London took all that Kentish soil had to offer and thus enriched the countryside, the towns of Kent declined. With the dissolution of the monasteries, Canterbury 'became in manner waste'. This was, in Protestant Lambarde's view, only just, because in such places, with their heavy complement of idolatrous monks, God was 'blasphemed most'. But other places had declined even without the handicap of God's wrath. Few of the Cinque Ports survived the competition of London and one of them ceased to be a port at all. At Romney, in Leland's words, 'within remembrance of men, ships have come hard up to the town and cast anchors in one of the church yards'. But now the sea was two miles away and the town 'so sore thereby now decayed', that in place of three great parish churches scarcely one was well maintained.

Kent, living in the shadow of the metropolis, brings us at last to London. Leland has almost nothing to say of it, but luckily we can find another guide, who wrote a generation later. This was John Stow, a Londoner born, who lived for 30 years as a working tailor, until his passion for literature and history became all-absorbing. In England, where devotion to the countryside has long been fashionable and successful business-men hurry to buy rural estates, few men have upheld the virtues of urban life. Stow was one of the few. Living in cities, he said, 'men by this nearness of conversation are withdrawn from barbarous ferity and force to a certain mildness of manners and to humanity and justice'. Stow's life-work, the *Survey of London*, was testimony to this belief.

We think of London today as a monolith; but in Stow's time it was grouped into two cities, Westminster and London, and a suburb, Southwark. Moving east down the Thames we come first to Westminster on our left. Here were buildings of the utmost architectural splendour. Furthest from the river lay the Abbey, financed by Henry III in a century of great artistic achievement and lately extended by Henry VII's chapel, with

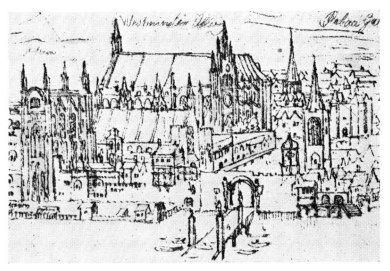

Westminster from the river, in 1558

its superb and extravagant fan-vaulting. To the north-east was Westminster Hall, built by the Norman kings as their largest palace, now converted into the main seat of government. In the body of this vast hall sat the three great courts of law: common pleas on the right-hand side near the entrance, king's bench further up on the same side, and chancery on the left at the far end. Arrangements were simple. In common pleas the judges sat on long raised benches, with their clerks below them, and great oaken planks running round the sides of the court to

form an enclosure for litigants and lawyers. Only in chancery
was there any sign of pomp, for here a marble chair and a
marble table were provided for the lord chancellor. Severely
practical though the arrangements were, there must have been
some confusion when three courts sat in the same hall, however
large it may have been.

Adjoining the hall were other offices of government, such as
the exchequer and the star chamber with its gilded ceiling, while
nearby was St Stephen's Chapel, once the private chapel of the
king and since 1548 the main seat of Parliament. To the south
lay the privy palace of the king, built for his household when
the hall itself became the home of public government. Here had
been the greatest royal residence of the Middle Ages, largely
destroyed by fire in 1512. Rather than rebuild it, Henry VIII
found another site to the north of Westminster Abbey, where
the Archbishops of York had long had a palace. On the fall of
his minister Cardinal Wolsey, who had greatly extended the
palace, Henry took it over for the crown and 'brought it,
by great expense, into its . . . princely form'. This form was
from the outside rather unimpressive. An Italian visitor of the
next century called it 'nothing more than an assemblage of

The Palace of Whitehall in 1560

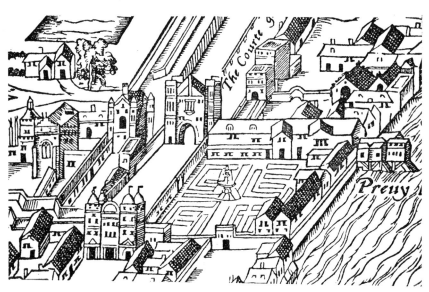

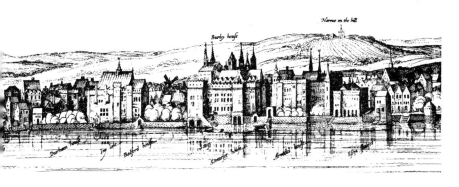

The houses of the great men, between the Strand and the River

several houses, badly built at different times and for different purposes'. Even within, it was disappointing when the monarch was not in residence: if Elizabeth was absent, wrote a German, 'all the fine tapestries are removed, so that nothing but the bare walls are to be seen'. But when she was there with her court, the scene was described by the Venetian ambassador as 'rather a Theatre Celestial than a Palace of Earthly Building'.

Behind and around Westminster there were few buildings. Tothill Fields, St Martin's Field, and Covent Garden were all, in Stow's day open spaces. But along the bank of the Thames, Westminster was linked to the City by a row of great houses with gardens running down from the Strand to the river's edge. At Ivy Bridge William Cecil had 'raised a large and stately house of brick and timber'; next came Russell House, belonging to the earl of Bedford; then the palace of the Savoy, long ago ruined and now used as a 'workhouse for the poor and idle persons'; then Somerset House; and finally Essex House, where Elizabeth's favourite made his last stand. Of them all, Somerset House survives; the others are commemorated in the names of streets and hotels.

Beyond Essex House the outskirts of the city led along Fleet Street and over the Fleet River to Ludgate, where began the wall which still enclosed that fantastic square mile of riches, the City of London. Here was conducted 80 per cent of the nation's foreign trade; here lived the arrogant merchants who behaved, in their rivals' words, 'as if God had no sons to whom He gave the benefit of the earth, but in London'. Apart from its churches the City had few impressive public buildings and

17

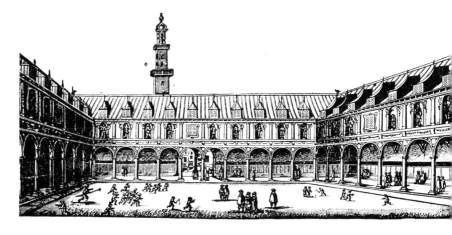

The Royal Exchange, built by Sir Thomas Gresham in 1566

there was nothing to rival the great central squares of continental towns like Siena. Only the Royal Exchange was architecturally remarkable. It was begun in 1566 when Sir Thomas Gresham and other aldermen each laid down a piece of gold upon the foundation-stone. These gold pieces were taken up by the workmen and so encouraged them that the whole building was finished in seventeen months. A few great men still had houses in the City: Thomas Cromwell, for instance, had encroached on the garden of Stow's father to put up a 'very large and spacious' building, causing Stow to comment sourly 'that the sudden rising of some men causeth them to forget themselves'. In Goldsmith's Row was the 'most beautiful frame of fair houses and shops that be within the walls of London'. But most of the houses seem to have been built rather for practical accommodation than for beauty or grandeur.

For the City was growing explosively and there was neither time nor space for leisurely

Archery practice at Moorfields

building. Estimates of London's population are uncertain; but it may well be that the City grew from about 60,000 in Leland's day to about a quarter of a million at the end of the century. Every possible plot of land was filled in, the sites of dissolved

18

monasteries being found especially useful. Then the City began to spread, in a ribbon-development, beyond its earlier limits. Eastwards from the Tower there grew, according to Stow, 'a continual street, or filthy straight passage, with alleys of small

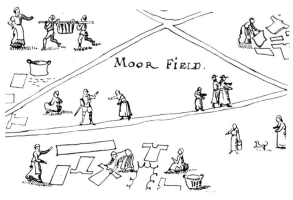

MOOR FIELD.

Spreading out washing to dry at Moorfields

tenements or cottages builded, inhabited by sailors' victuallers, along by the river of Thames, almost to Radcliffe'. Even so, the countryside was still nearby. Just north of the city wall, where Liverpool Street Station now stands, was the district of Moorfields, too damp and spongy for easy building. Here Londoners came to lay out their laundry, to milk their cattle, to practise archery, or simply to walk and talk.

South of the river was Southwark, with its rows of tenements, its inns, and its places of entertainment. Stow tells us of its 'two bear gardens, the old and new places', where 'these bears and other beasts are there baited in plots of ground, scaffolded about for the beholders to stand safe'. But inhibited by his religious conscience, he says nothing of its three theatres, among them the famous Globe, carefully sited outside the City boundaries in order to escape suppression by the puritan-minded Mayor and Corporation.

Linking Westminster, Southwark and the City was the Thames, 'a sure and most beautiful road for shipping'. There was then only one bridge over the river, London Bridge, and most people preferred to travel by boat, whether they wished to cross from one bank to another, or whether they wished to move up or down stream. Roads were narrow,

South-bank entertainment

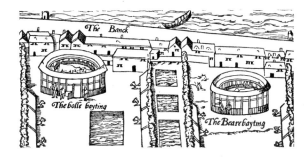

The Thames and the City in 1600, from St Paul's on the

bumpy, and dirty; the river way was smooth and quick, though probably no cleaner. In consequence there were on Stow's reckoning 2,000 wherries and other small boats plying for hire. Not that the crossing was always easy, for the Thames was a place of sport as well as a highway. The unfortunate secretary of Archbishop Cranmer, going by wherry from Westminster to the City, passed by the royal barge, 'with a great number of barges and boats about him, then baiting of bears in the water'. His boat was soon firmly wedged among the other wherries and barges, so that 'there was no refuge if the bear should break loose and come upon them, as, in very deed, within one paternoster while, the bear brake loose; and came into the boat'. The poor man's wherry began to sink and he himself was pushed out of it by the bear. At this point, not before time, Henry VIII ended proceedings with the words 'Away, away, with the bear! and let us all go hence!'.

Sometimes the entertainments on the Thames were rather more decorous. On 29th May 1533 every company of the City took its barge to Greenwich, 'with goodly banners fresh and new', and 'minstrels making great and sweet harmony'. At

20

left (without its spire which had collapsed) to London Bridge

three o'clock Queen Anne Boleyn entered her barge and the whole company set off to Tower Wharf, saluted by ordnance from ships in the river. There she was greeted by the king, before the eyes of the largest crowd ever seen, 'that stood on the shore on both sides of the river'.

London has had the largest place in this survey, and deservedly so. For the City's commerce gave dynamic impetus to the cloth-makers and the wool-growers of the countryside; the law-courts and the Parliament at Westminster commanded the attention of the ruling classes; the theatres of Southwark and the suburbs were the scene of great literary triumphs; and the court of the monarchs provided a symbol of unity and a fountain of patronage. But this urban greatness stood alone in England. The next town to London in size was Norwich, with a population of about 20,000; and most other important boroughs, like Shrewsbury and Exeter, fell below 10,000. England was still a land of farms, manor-houses, villages, and market towns; even its main industry, the weaving of cloth, was mostly conducted in the countryside.

The land itself had not much changed since the early Middle Ages. Great areas of hill and moor were still unoccupied and uncultivated; the open-field system of agriculture persisted over most of central England; transport and travel were difficult; and many regions lived in isolation from the rest of the country. Such isolation was most obvious on the fringes: men of the northernmost shires felt themselves to be borderers above all else; Welshmen and Cornishmen resented the intrusion of the English; the fen-dwellers were regarded as a race apart. But throughout the realm, regional differences were strongly marked: farming systems varied widely; local customs were strongly defended; and everywhere a man's first loyalty lay within his county.

Further Reading

John Leland, *The Itinerary* (ed. L. Toulmin Smith), 1906-10
John Stow, *A Survey of London* (ed. C. L. Kingsford), 1908
A. L. Rowse, *The England of Elizabeth*, 1950
— —, *The Expansion of Elizabethan England*, 1950
W. G. Hoskins, *Midland England*, 1949
Joan Thirsk, *Fenland Farming in the Sixteenth Century*, 1953
C. M. L. Bouch and G. P. Jones, *The Lake Counties, 1500-1830*, 1961
G. Dyfnallt Owen, *Elizabethan Wales*, 1962
A. L. Rowse, *Tudor Cornwall*, 1941
R. J. Mitchell and M. D. R. Leys, *A History of London Life*, 1958

II

Trade, Industry and Agriculture

To men of the mid-sixteenth century the root cause of all the changes in their time seemed to be the rise in prices, which began in England around 1500, accelerated sharply in the 1540s, moved more slowly after 1550, and then shot forward again in the last decade of the century. Since some goods increased in price much more than others it is impossible to give any accurate quantitative assessment of the rise. But one can reasonably say that the food and other goods needed by an artisan family cost, by the end of the century, something like five times as much as they had cost at the beginning. This was decidedly less rapid than the inflation with which we have been living since 1939; but to men who believed that there was a single just price for everything it seemed both monstrous and shocking. One northcountryman was so alarmed by it that he carved on the front of his house: 'this house was builded in the fourth year of the reign of King Edward the sixth, when a bushel of wheat was at 7s., a bushel of beer a noble [6s. 8d.], malt 3s. and more'. Bishop Latimer spoke of 'such dearth, that poor men, which live of their labour, cannot with the sweat of their face have a living, all kind of victuals is so dear'. 'If it thus continue.' he said, 'we shall at length be constrained to pay for a pig a pound'.

Why did prices rise? Even in an age as statistically minded as our own this is not an easy question to answer convincingly, for the personal bias of the economist often decides his choice of explanations. In the sixteenth century, barren of statistics, the answer is still harder to find. Traditionally historians have thought that the principal causes of the inflation were the influx of bullion from the New World and the debasement of the coinage by Henry VIII. While American bullion had its effect upon Spain, there is no evidence that enough of it entered England to bring about a major rise in prices here. The debasement of the currency certainly depressed the value of money, but cannot by itself account for the scale of the inflation. Nor does the pattern of the change in price-levels suggest that monetary causes alone were at work: the price of foodstuffs rose much more rapidly than the price of manufactures, suggesting that shortage of food may have been at least as important a cause of inflation as excess of money.

Why should food have been short? The most probable explanation is that population was rising and that there were more mouths to feed. Unfortunately there is no direct evidence that population rose, although a good deal of circumstantial evidence points in that direction. Contemporary views on the subject conflicted. Thomas Starkey, writing in the 1530s, pointed to the declining towns and deserted villages, in order to show that population, far from increasing, had fallen. The houses that were 'ruined and decayed' and the ground which 'lyeth as barren or to the nourishing of wild beasts' declared to his mind a 'great lack of people and scarseness of men'. But by the reign of Elizabeth a rise in population had become apparent to Richard Hakluyt, who claimed in 1584 'that through our long peace and seldom sickness we are grown more populous than ever heretofore'. The Cornishman, Richard Carew, also spoke of an increase in population in his own county. He put it down to clerical marriage—'the banishment of single-living votaries'—and to 'younger marriages than of old', as well as to 'our long freedom from any forewasting war or plague'.

It is strange that one man should see a fall, others a rise in population. But there is an explanation for this difference of opinion, which seems plausible enough. The generally held

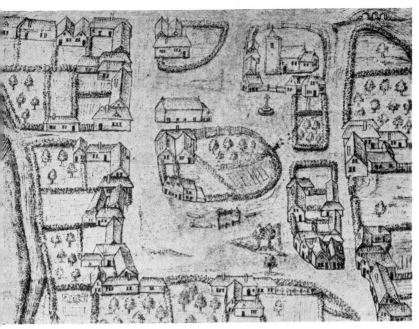

The layout of a village in the late Middle Ages

view that the families of rural England stayed in one village from generation to generation, from century to century, is for the sixteenth century almost entirely false. In south Nottinghamshire, for instance, most freeholders held their lands for less than two generations; and the region does not seem to be at all unusual in this respect. Some classes of men were always on the move, and the muster-masters found difficulty in parading for the militia 'servants and artificers which . . . change and remove their dwellings daily'. Moreover, the economic forces of the time helped some communities and ruined others. The decay of a town or village was plain to see in its fallen and deserted houses. The growing population of others was, in its earlier stages, harder to take in. But such growth probably outweighed the decline elsewhere.

Since much of this increase in population came within the towns, which did not produce wool or food, the price of these raw materials naturally rose. At the same time, the amount of cultivable land available for each member of the population was reduced by the general growth in numbers, creating an intense and uneasy hunger for land, with a consequent rise in rents. Thus an inflationary spiral was set off, with rents, food prices, and wool prices pulling each other upwards.

The rise in prices and the growth in population were not confined to England alone, and their progress on the European mainland helped to quicken English trade. In the fourteenth century the great foundation of our commerce had been the export of raw wool by the Company of the Staple through Calais: 'of Brutus' Albion his wool is chief richesse', wrote Lydgate. But by the beginning of the Tudor period the Company of Merchant Adventurers had built up a trade in manufactured woollen cloth to rival this earlier predominance of the Staplers. With the expansion of the European economy, this export of cloth grew by 150 per cent during the first half of the sixteenth century. As the exports in cloth rose, the wool trade naturally sank, carrying with it the town of Calais and several of the smaller English ports. Their decline saw the rise of London to commercial supremacy in England and the growing

A casualty of the declining wool trade: the town and port of Calais

dependence of our trade upon the great cosmopolitan market of Antwerp. As a Flemish proverb put it: 'if Englishmen's fathers were hanged at Antwerp's gates, their children, to come into that town, would creep betwixt their legs'. In 1551 the Antwerp market began to crumble, until by 1575 it had almost entirely collapsed. The main prop of our economy had gone. To begin with, English merchants could

A merchant ship

still hope for some profit from the traditional commerce in wine with Bordeaux and in wool, fruit, and oil with Spain. But before long these trades too had been severely damaged in the wars of the Elizabethan era, and merchants had to look further afield. Luckily the build of sailing ships had already developed far enough to make this possible. In the course of the fifteenth century the single mast typical of the Middle Ages had been replaced by two masts or more, the use of lateen sails on the aftermasts had begun, and ships' hulls had become longer and more seaworthy. Improvements in design continued during the Tudor period with the appearance of top-sails and top-masts.

Bristol ships pushed their way into the Newfoundland fishing banks, while east-coast vessels fought with Scots and Germans 'for the primacy and privilege of the Iceland ports to ride in'—for Icelandic fisheries were then, as they are now, a battleground. Others were still more adventurous. Except for the isolated voyages of the Cabots, England had taken little part in the earliest European explorations; but from the reign of Henry VIII her sailors began to follow the great explorers of France, Portugal, and Spain. William Hawkins and Thomas Wyndham sailed the coast of Africa. Frobisher and Gilbert tried to find a way through the north-west passage to China. Willoughby and Chancellor pushed through the

27

White Sea to the mouth of the Dvina and to Moscow. Anthony Jenkinson, one of the most articulate of Elizabethan travellers, followed them there and went on to Bokhara, whence he sent a disappointing report that, although 'there is yearly a great resort of merchants to this city', these merchants 'are so beggarly and poor . . . that there is no hope of any good trade'.

The explorations were followed by organised commerce. The Russia Company traded with Moscow, the Barbary Company with Morocco, the Levant Company with the Near East, while William Hawkins' son John started the profitable slave-trade between England and Spanish America. But glamorous as these enterprises were, much as they had in their bones the feel of the future, they were, in the Tudor period, only a minor part of English trade. For the great bulk of our exports still went in cloth to the ports of northern Europe, and the monopolistic market of Antwerp had now been replaced by Middelburg, Stade, Emden, and Hamburg. Once the great boom in the English cloth trade was over, there followed a time of recovery and consolidation under the young Elizabeth and then, at the end of the century, an

28

Part of Anthony Jenkinson's map of Russia, Muscovy and Tartary, 1562

attempt to develop the manufacture and export of lighter cloth, known as the 'new draperies'.

The growth and fluctuations of commerce naturally had their effects upon English industry. With the increasing demand for cloth in the fifteenth century, the manufacture of textiles expanded and changed its character.

An early Tudor merchant

Originally cloth-making had been centred in such substantial towns as York, Coventry, Norwich, and Salisbury. But during the fifteenth century entrepreneurs were building up their industry in country districts, perhaps in order to escape the restrictive practices of the urban guilds. In the new textile villages the weavers worked on a domestic system; though nominally independent, they were in practice the wage-labourers of the clothiers who supplied them with raw materials and sometimes with looms. In the first half of the sixteenth century booming exports encouraged the industry to expand its capacity still further.

Wool-growing attracted landlords and farmers, while the looms provided occupation for men who could no longer make a living on the land. The economy was dangerously dependent on this single commodity, rather as until 1939 South Wales depended upon coal and Tyneside upon shipbuilding, so that, when the crash came on the Antwerp market in 1551, the country was badly shaken. Industrialists, labourers, and wool-growers all suffered. The second half of the century saw

The arms of the Company of Mines Royal, 1568

29

Miners at work

a gradual recovery until the high levels of the earlier period were almost regained; but the mood now was cautious and restrained.

The dominance of the cloth-industry was to some extent offset in the course of the sixteenth century by the development of other concerns. The making of salt from sea-water became a major industry at Shields on the Tyne and later produced the smoke that Defoe, from a distance of sixteen miles, saw 'ascend in huge clouds over the hills'. John Evelyn's grandfather was given a monopoly for making gun-powder. Blast furnaces for making iron were set up on the Weald. German miners were brought over to dig for copper in Cumberland and for calamine in Somerset. Above all, the output of English coal-mines increased eight-fold in the hundred years between 1540 and 1640.

It is difficult to assess the impact of all these changes on the life of the sixteenth century. To contemporaries the rise in prices, the expansion of trade, and the appearance of new industries appeared momentous, and to some historians they have seemed

30

comparable to the economic transformation of the eighteenth century. Lately there has been some reaction against these views. It has been pointed out, perfectly rightly, that the rate of inflation was modest by current standards, that the growth of commerce was halted in mid-century, that the development of new industries, spectacular as it might seem, started from so low a level that their contribution to the economy remained small. English industry and trade did not, in their main features and emphasis, markedly alter in the course of the sixteenth century, for cloth export was still the staple of the economy. Above all England remained primarily a farming, not an industrial, nation. But although English society preserved much of its traditional structure throughout the sixteenth century there were nevertheless important changes in the lives and attitudes of its members. These changes are the subject of this book.

The rise in prices, the growing number of mouths to feed, and the reiterated demands of the clothiers for wool put great opportunities and great pitfalls in the way of English landowners and peasants. The man who lived on a fixed income, the labourer who had to buy food at ever-rising prices, the smallholder whose land was coveted by a more powerful neighbour, all these stood to lose. But men with secure titles and land enough to produce a surplus of food or a quantity of wool had the chance to prosper.

How were they to turn the opportunity for gain into gain itself? One method, that of the small farmer, was thrifty and efficient application of the old ways. The sixteenth century saw no great changes in farming techniques, certainly nothing to compare with the introduction of turnips in the eighteenth century. The farming year and the methods of agriculture remained much as they had always been. For over a great part of England the open-field system of agriculture prevailed throughout the century. Round the village were the three great stretches of arable land, with crops rotating from one to another, generally in three-yearly cycles. In the first field the peasants would sow winter corn—wheat or rye; in the second spring seeds—barley, oats, beans or peas; and in the third the land

31

The open-field village: Boarstall in Buckinghamshire

would lie fallow. The winter corn would have been sown between Lammas Day, August 1st, and Hallowmass, November 1st. It would be harvested in the following July or the first two weeks of August. The spring crops would have been sown between February and Easter, except for barley which was sown a little later, and would be reaped with the winter corn. After harvest the fences around these two fields could be removed and the livestock allowed to graze there until the next sowing. The third, and fallow, field would have been ploughed three times between March and July in preparation for its sowing of wheat or rye in the following autumn. The first field would then be got ready for the next sowing of spring crops and the second field would lie fallow. These arable lands were divided into strips of many shapes and sizes, in a patchwork. In different counties the strips had different names: 'rigs' in Lincolnshire, 'dales' in Westmorland, 'selions' in Nottinghamshire, and so on. Each peasant had his land scattered in these strips among the three great fields, so that each might have his due proportion of winter corn, spring corn, and fallow.

In the low-lying land of the village were some of its most valuable plots, the meadows, fenced off for growing hay from Candlemas, February 2nd, until midsummer. Beyond the arable fields lay the unploughed wastes of the common pastures and woodlands, on which the flocks and herds of the commoner grazed together when the arable was under crop or ready for seed. Such in brief, crude outline, ignoring many local variations and changes brought about by time, was the open-field system between the thirteenth century and the sixteenth.

The disadvantages of such a system were striking: one-third of all the arable was wasted every year by lying fallow; there was no winter feed available for the livestock, whose numbers had therefore to be reduced at the beginning of winter; the killing of this livestock meant that too little manure went into the ground; and the common system of agriculture allowed the backward and incompetent to hinder the efficient. There was little that could be done about most of these drawbacks until the use of turnips and clover brought in a four-course rotation and provided winter feed for the animals. But at least there was a chance for the go-ahead man. Printing opened up to him one line of improvement, for, in the course of the sixteenth century, there was published a series of handbooks on farming methods. The first of these, by John Fitzherbert or his brother Sir Anthony, was a serious and detailed work, *The Booke of Husbandrye*. Fitzherbert went very carefully into techniques of ploughing, describing the ploughs most suitable for different soils, pointing out that oxen would plough in tough clay where

Ploughing with oxen

Fitzherbert on ploughing

horses would not move, that horses by contrast went faster on even ground. The farmer's wife must not be idle: she should pray on first getting out of bed, then clean the house, dress the dishboard, milk the cows, suckle the calves, dress her children, cook meals for the household, bake and brew when needed, send corn to the mill, make butter and cheese, look after the swine, and collect the eggs. The author's earnest and industrious tone can be seen from this exhausting catalogue. Characteristically he devoted his final chapter to advice on heavenly riches, and then told a young gentleman wishing to thrive that 'I advise him to get a copy of this present book and to read it from the beginning to the ending', a frank piece of self-advertisement that many authors might copy if modern conventions did not inhibit them.

Fitzherbert's successor, Thomas Tusser, published his *Hundreth Good Pointes of Husbandrie* in 1557. The book was an instant success, went into several editions and was later expanded into *Five Hundred* points of husbandry and another *Five Hundred* points of housewifery. Tusser's book, written in jogging couplets, is altogether a more lively and relaxed affair than Fitzherbert's, but no more than his predecessor does he suggest any great advances in agricultural method. What the reader got from Tusser was sound common-sense application of the old ways.

> *Get ever before hand, drag never behind,*
> *Lest winter beclip thee and break of thy mind.*

Advice which most of us might take to heart for our gardens!

His remarks on the servant problem may, however, be less apt for the present day.

> *Keep never such servants as doth thee no good*
> *For making thy hair groweth thorough thy hood;*
> *For nestling of varlets, of brothels, and whores,*
> *Make many a rich man to shut up his doors.*

But he could be more cheerful. When harvest was in the farmer was told

> *Then welcome thy harvest folk, servants and all*
> *With mirth and good cheer let them furnish the hall.*

His advice on harvest celebrations recalls the description by a German traveller: 'their last load of corn they crown with flowers, having besides an image richly dressed, by which perhaps they would signify Ceres.' Tusser can at least remind us that verse has a respectable and forgotten practical function, below the level of great poetry. Is not Tusser, to be frank, much more readable than a great deal of Sir Thomas Wyatt?

Not that such books made all that difference to farming. The most they can have done is to make the best of traditional methods more widely known and practised. Probably enclosure was more helpful to the intelligent peasant than printing. The

Harvesting

Harvest home

word 'enclosure' has of course a sinister ring, for reasons that we shall see later; but it took many forms, of which one, the joining together and fencing off of arable strips, had long been practised to the advantage of farmers. The notion that the medieval village was an unchanging unit has recently been disproved, for during the later Middle Ages peasants were constantly buying, selling, and exchanging land, and enclosure of part of the arable for temporary pasture was very common. From the middle of the fourteenth century the more energetic farmers had been increasing and consolidating their arable holdings, while fencing off part of the common for separate use. Most progressive writers approved of such enclosure. Fitzherbert said that it was better for the farmer to keep livestock in fenced closes than to 'have his cattle go before the herdman'—that is, to be driven by the village herdsman onto the common. Tusser approved of enclosed arable:

The country enclosed I praise,
The other delighteth not me,
For nothing the wealth it does raise
To such as inferior be.

Threshing with flails

Certainly these developments gave the chance to the better farmer to improve his land and his stock; and the chance was taken. The Reverend William Harrison, writing early in the reign of Elizabeth, said that 'certainly it [the soil] is even now in these our days grown to be much more fruitful than it hath been in times past'.

36

To landlords such methods seemed perhaps too slow to save them from the painful squeeze of higher prices. Having mostly leased out their demesne lands in the course of the fifteenth century, they depended largely on rents for their income. But leases made before the time of inflation were easily eroded by rising prices and served only as obstacles in the way of the new possibilities of profit. Landlords near London wished to take advantage of the prosperity that might come from food production, while their colleagues elsewhere hoped to benefit from the high price and low production costs of wool. To all such men the traditional structure of fixed rents, common pastures, and open-field arable was simply a hindrance to be demolished. The lines of attack adopted by landlords depended very much on the region in which their estates lay. In some places enclosure of the commons seemed the best answer; in others conversion of arable to pasture; and in others again the raising of rents.

Parks of the gentry in Rutlandshire

Such considerations lay behind the enclosure movement of the late fifteenth and sixteenth centuries. The term 'enclosure' meant, as I have said, many things. In the first place it referred to the process, already described, of consolidating strips in the arable and thus improving the productivity of the soil. This was usually harmless enough; but there were more sinister types. One, known sometimes as 'imparking', sprang less from the urge to profit than from the landlord's desire for that essential item of prestige, a deer-park. Elizabethan maps of the English shires are careful to show these newly fenced-off status symbols.

37

A shepherd

Another type involved the destruction of common rights and the reservation of large parts of the grazing to the growing flocks of the landlord. Some of those flocks were certainly very large: Sir Richard Southwell of Wood Rising in Norfolk had fourteen flocks, averaging over one thousand sheep apiece, and they needed all the pastures that they could get. Often the possibilities of the commons were not enough and the landlord then turned his attention to the available arable. Plots were 'engrossed' by him, strips consolidated, and the land put down to pasture.

Such in brief and abstract terms was the process. What it often meant in practice can be seen from the petition to Henry VIII of the villagers of Westangmering in Sussex, against their landlord, John Palmer. He had, they alleged, 'spoiled, destroyed, and pulled down some of the houses of your said poor subjects and the timber thereof hath given away'; he caused some of them by compulsion 'to take other lands, being none of his own, in other places further off at his pleasure, being worse lands'; and he sent his servants to beat and threaten those who would not obey him. All this is of course accusation. But while it may not be true of Palmer himself, it illustrates what was often happening, and there is, in any case, the ring of truth in a snatch of recorded dialogue. One of the peasant wives asked Palmer: 'Jesu, sir, in the name of God, what mean you thus extremely to handle us poor people?' To this Palmer replied: 'Do ye not know that the King's grace hath put down all the houses of monks, friars, and nuns? Therefore now is the time come that we gentlemen will pull down the houses of such poor knaves as ye be.'

We do not know Palmer's object in enclosing this land. But there is little doubt that many landlords at this time were

38

encroaching on the common pasture or converting arable land to grass in order to build up their flocks of sheep. The consequent disruption of rural society is well known from the protests made at the time. 'Your sheep', wrote Sir Thomas More, 'that were wont to be so meek and tame, and so small eaters, now, as I hear say, be become so great devourers and so wild, that they eat up, and swallow down the very men themselves'. With sharp and angry irony More described how nobles and gentlemen, 'yea and certain abbots, holy men no doubt', enclose their land for pasture, 'pluck down towns [i.e. villages], and leave nothing standing but only a church to be made a sheephouse'. The words of this scholarly man were widely echoed in more popular literature:

> *The towns go down, the land decays:*
> *Of cornfields plain leys,*
> *Great men maketh now-a-days*
> *A sheepcot in the church.*
> *Commons to close and keep,*
> *Poor folk for bread to cry and weep*
> *Towns pulled down to pasture sheep,*
> *This is the new guise.*

Visible evidence for these effects of enclosure is to be found over much of England, especially midland England, in the sites of deserted villages. Aerial photographs, old maps, and careful digging have revealed places where villages stood in medieval times and were gone by the middle of the sixteenth century. One such was Wharram Percy in Yorkshire; another was the village of Whatborough in Leicestershire, destroyed by the prior of Launde in 1494. These were not isolated examples. Writing at the end of the fifteenth century, the antiquary John Rous attacked the 'destruction of villages which brings dearth to the common-

Whatborough village, in a map of 1576

39

wealth', named 58 villages in Warwickshire that had disappeared, and concluded that 'if such destructions as that in
Warwickshire took place in other parts of the country, it
would be a national danger'. John Rous's academic descendants,
led by Professor M. W. Beresford, have identified 56 of
his lost Warwickshire villages and have located more than 100
deserted villages in Lincolnshire.

The destruction of most of these villages seems to have
occurred between about 1440 and 1520. Perhaps in its earlier
stages it resulted from the agrarian depression of the late
fourteenth century, rather than the boom of the early sixteenth.
In the thirteenth century, England had been by the standards
of the day a densely populated country marked by hunger for
land. New villages were being built, some of them on poor soil.
With the famines of Edward II's reign, the Black Death of his
son's, and the endemic plague of the years that followed,
many of these new sites were deserted. The survivors of
calamity probably moved to more attractive fields. This retreat
from the marginal lands was succeeded by a retreat from arable
farming. With fewer mouths to feed and wages high, wool
farming seemed to many landlords a better proposition than
grain production. Then, gradually, the market for cloth began

Wharram Percy, Yorkshire, as revealed by a map of 1850 and an aerial photograph

to boom, and wool offered, not just a better way out of the impasse than grain, but a positive and expanding inducement. Landlords who could manage it turned over to pasture and evicted their tenants from the arable in order to do so. Thus a movement of depopulation that began with the retreat from marginal land swept on with the eviction of peasant farmers to make way for sheep.

Landlord and tenant

Enclosure was not the only resort of the landlord or richer farmer who was pressed by rising prices and saw the opportunities of the market. Pamphlets and sermons castigate the rich for 'engrossing' and 'rent-raising' almost as often as they attack them for enclosure. 'Engrossing' can roughly be defined as the joining together of two or more farms, thus creating a larger and more productive unit, but providing a living for only one family. The rich yeoman or gentleman-farmer was able in this way to extend his acres, while the unsuccessful had to become wage-labourers or to join the army of displaced poor.

Many landlords found their rents utterly inadequate after prices had risen. Some pieces of land were held by copyholders, whose annual rents had been fixed a century or more ago and could not legally be raised; other pieces were held by tenants on long leases at rents that could only be raised at wide intervals. The landlord was therefore in the uncomfortable position familiar to anyone who tries to live upon a fixed income in times of inflation. 'In all my life time', said one of them, 'I look not that the third part of my land shall come to my disposition, that I may enhance the rent of the same; but it shall be in men's holdings either by lease or by copy granted before my time.' Replying to the merchants who complained of the rising price of wool, he said: 'we cannot raise all our wares as you may yours'.

41

However, the landlord had his resources. He might not be able to raise a copyholder's annual rent, but when the copyholder died he could put up the 'fine-on-entry' or 'gressum', the premium that a tenant's heir had to pay to the landlord before he could inherit the tenancy. These premiums were fixed by convention, often at one or two years' rent. But convention could be overcome if there was enough competition for the tenancy, and this competition was provided by the rising population. Cornish copyholds with traditional fines of £1 or £2 were now bringing in premiums of £30 or £50.

The same competition was driving up the rents of leasehold land, allowing an economic or 'rack' rent to be charged. Richard Carew described the rush for land in Cornwall: 'for a farm . . . can no sooner fall in hand, than the survey court shall be waited on with many officers, vying and re-vying each on other; nay, they are mostly taken at a ground-hop, for fear of coming too late.' It is a vivid picture of the rush of prospective tenants. George Owen, the Pembrokeshire antiquary, writing like Carew at the end of the century, tells of the misfortune of the leaseholder: 'now the poor tenant that lived well in that golden world is taught to sing unto his lord a new song. . . . He standeth so in bodily fear of his greedy neighbour that two or three years ere his lease end, he must bow to his lord for a new lease, and must pinch it out many years before to heap money together.'

Was the outcry against 'rack-renting' and enclosure justified by the facts? In defence of the landlords it has been argued that rents rose no faster than prices; but it is unlikely that this was true of the whole country. Whether or not they kept ahead of prices, they certainly rose very sharply. For the go-ahead farmer, for the yeoman with plenty of food or wool to sell, this may not have mattered: he produced more at better prices. For the small man, or for the inefficient, it may well have been disastrous. The copyholder was no longer protected against higher fines on entry, and if he could not pay them he would be removed and the land converted to leasehold. By contrast with the conservative and leisurely life of the past, the English farming routine was now in part based upon the rigorous demands of economic survival.

The impact of enclosure varied from one region to another. In the marshland of the Lincolnshire coast, pasture was already ample and there was no point in laying down more land to grass; but in the Midlands profit could be and was made by converting the predominantly arable fields into grazing for

A country estate: Burrowes Hall, Cheshire in 1576

sheep or cattle. It has been argued that landlords were not really so voracious as the pamphleteers insisted, that the amount of land enclosed was small, that enclosure helped the soil, and that large farms formed more efficient units. It is difficult to assess the weights of these claims, for it is now quite clear that many of the statistics so laboriously totted up by propagandists and historians are worthless. But one can say this. Although

43

A labourer

there is much to be urged on behalf of the landlords, it is just not true that all enclosures benefited the soil, nor that the small proportion of land involved meant an unharmed peasantry. For men and communities living on the edge of survival quite a small disturbance of their livelihood might be the end. Reduction of their commons would make them cut down their flocks; and fewer animals meant less manure for arable land that was already underfed. In some areas, especially the Midland clays and the Cotswold uplands, the disruption and the suffering were real.

Not that the peasants were defenceless. Many of them had strongly entrenched legal rights. The landlord might be able to eject without much ado his tenants-at-will, but copyholders were far more secure. Their position varied from that of the tenant for inheritance, who could hardly be removed, to that of the tenant for life, whose heirs could be kept out by a careful landlord. Much depended upon the skill and the scruples of the landlord, the precise titles upon which tenancies were held, and the determination of the peasants. In a small, poor village resistance was not likely to be vigorous; and no doubt the villages lost to the world were mostly of this kind. Larger villages, especially those with some richer peasants, had a better chance. A common purse could be collected, advice taken, lawyers employed, and the landlord fought in the courts, often with success.

For the law-courts were not entirely on the side of the ruling class. The Tudor monarchs and their advisers saw with concern the changes in the countryside, the decay of farmhouses, the growing mass of poor. The peasants who formed the backbone of the army were being lost, and their discontent might lead to riot. From the early years of Henry VII, statutes and proclamations attempted to limit the changes. Landlords must not turn

44

arable to pasture; they must not pull down farmhouses. In short, they must preserve the old order.

No one familiar with the well-meaning but ramshackle machinery of Tudor government could believe it capable of halting for long a process urged on by economic forces and determined men. Yet it did something. Peasants 'complained without number' to the Tudor courts. Sometimes they got redress; sometimes perhaps a landlord was brought to hesitate before enclosing. The general change may not have been arrested; but some individual hardships may have been mitigated or prevented.

Further Reading

P. Ramsey, *Tudor Economic Problems*, 1963
G. D. Ramsay, *English Overseas Trade*, 1957
R. H. Tawney, *The Agrarian Problem in the Sixteenth Century*, 1912
Joan Thirsk, *Tudor Enclosures*, 1959
M. W. Beresford, *The Lost Villages of England*, 1954

III

The Order of Society

'Where order lacketh,' said Sir Thomas Elyot, 'there all thing is odious and uncomely.' He was voicing the common assumption of his age that there was a divinely ordained hierarchy of being from the Almighty at the top, down through the angels and men to the brute beasts, and that only by the preservation of this natural order could primeval chaos be averted. Shakespeare's Ulysses put the point with theatrical force in *Troilus and Cressida*:

> *Take but degree away, untune that string*
> *And, hark, what discord follows!*

Henry VII: a man like other men

Early in the reign of Elizabeth, the Reverend William Harrison, rector of Radwinter in Essex, wrote a *Description of England*, called by himself 'this foul frizzled treatise of mine'. There were in England, he said, four sorts of men: gentlemen, merchants and burgesses, yeomen, and 'artificers and labourers'. We may well adopt him as our guide to English society and take these categories one by one. Yet first a warning: Harrison was talking of the orders of society, based upon status and birth, not of social classes based upon income, economic interest, and consciousness of a common cause. To suppose

46

anything else is dangerously misleading. There were, he said,
two classes of gentleman: 'the
first and chief (next the king) be
the prince, dukes, marquises, earls,
viscounts, and barons: and these
are called gentlemen of the greater
sort; ... next unto them be
knights, esquires and last of all
they that are simply called gentlemen.' Harrison put first in his
hierarchy the king, and we may
well begin at that point, with the
monarch and the court. The early
Tudor court came to be, in a new
sense, the centre of national life.
Stimulated by the renaissance
courts of men like Charles VIII
and Francis I of France, Henry VII
and his son developed an elaborate
ceremonial structure which was
both a focus and a symbol in
English politics, society, and
culture. With the growing power
of the State and the gradual

Henry VIII: a monarch as demi-god

disappearance of the over-mighty subject, the royal court
became the fountain of power and prestige.

At the head of society stood the king, his stature and magnificence constantly extended and emphasised by legislation,
propaganda, and portraiture. The king described by Stephen
Gardiner as representing the image of God upon earth was
painted by Holbein in much the same role. Portraits of Henry
VII show a man like other men; they reflect the growing
renaissance interest in the individual face and character.
Contrast with these the later Holbein pictures of Henry VIII!
The great wall-painting at Whitehall made the spectator feel
'abashed, annihilated in his presence', and even the cartoon, all
that remains of this masterpiece, can show us why. This

47

Elizabeth I: the symbolic portrait of a sovereign

tradition of royal portraits, which culminated in the great picture of Elizabeth standing on the map of England, set out to present the monarch, not as he was—few pictures of the elderly Elizabeth bear any relation to the dispassionate remarks of foreign observers—but as he ought to be. Pose and costume submerge the individual; portrait is replaced by icon.

To match this conception of the god-like king the early Tudor monarchs elaborated the complex structure of their court. The small court of medieval kings, wandering from one royal manor to another in search of food, was replaced by a far larger organisation based for much of the year upon a few royal palaces, from which summer progresses could be mounted. The rooms of these palaces were arranged in an ever-narrowing hierarchy—rather like Tudor society itself. First came the great Hall, open to many; behind it the Great Chamber, which gave into the Presence Chamber; and behind that again the Privy Chamber, to which access was carefully guarded. Thus there was an inner sanctum, reserved for the king and those closest to him, and an outer arena where all entitled to attend the court could hope for a sight of the monarch. Administering the court were two great offices: the department of the Lord Steward, headed in practice by the Treasurer and the Comptroller of the Household, looked after the food and drink; the department of the Lord Chamberlain supervised ceremonial and gave to the court its distinctive tone. The entertainments arranged by the Lord Chamberlain's department included theatrical performances, and the royal court thus came to be a centre of Elizabethan drama. To some extent of course the tone of court ceremonial varied with the personality of the monarch, and it is usual to regard the court of Henry VII as somewhat austere, that of Henry VIII as colourful and magnificent. But the financial accounts of Henry VII enable us to build up a rather different picture. We find him giving 'to one that brought the king a lion, in reward £2 13s. 4d.', 'to him that had had his bull baited, in reward 10s.', and finally to 'the young damsel that danceth, £30'. Thirty pounds would have been an enormous sum in those days just for dancing; perhaps she did more. At the wedding celebrations of Prince Arthur in 1501 a vast entertainment was given in Westminster Hall. 'Two marvellous mounts or mountains right cunningly practized' were drawn on, the first 'planted full of fresh trees', the second 'like unto a rock scorched and burned', with precious metals growing out of it. On the first sat 13 lords and knights, on the second 12 ladies, who got down and danced when the 'mountains' came to a halt.

Under Henry's successors such pageantry and magnificence were well maintained. But to emphasise the grandeur and the pantomime would be to miss something else, best described by Henry Howard, Earl of Surrey, in his poem about his upbringing at Windsor. Sadly remembering the days of his youth at court, he talks of

> The stately seats, the ladies bright of hue,
> The dances short, long tales of great delight,

and of

> The void walls eke, that harbour'd us each night:
> Wherewith, alas, reviveth in my breast
> The sweet accord, such sleeps as yet delight,
> The pleasant dreams, the quiet bed of rest,
> The secret thoughts imparted with such trust,
> The wanton talk, the divers change of play;
> The friendship sworn, each promise kept so just,
> Wherewith we passed the winter night away.

The royal court was not only the fountain of patronage; not

The nobleman as warrior: Richard Beauchamp jousting

only the seat of ceremonial and display: for the English landed classes it was boarding-school, university, club and London season.

The great nobles of early Tudor England were much like their medieval predecessors. Their life was passed in the midst of the vast families that made up their households, organised in imitation of the royal court, which was indeed thought 'requisite to be the mirror of others'. Some of these others were certainly huge. There were 166 persons in the service of the fifth earl of Northumberland, arranged in strict hierarchy under the four chief officers, the Chamberlain, the Steward, the Treasurer, and the Comptroller. Many of the leading officers were men of rank, sometimes related to the lord himself. The fourth earl of Northumberland, in Skelton's words

> . . . Had both day and night,
> Knights and squires, at every season when
> He called upon them, as menial household men.

Apart from the gentlemanly officers, most great households contained the young sons of other nobles, sent there either as wards of the lord or as pages to learn the ways of an aristocrat. In Cardinal Wolsey's household there was 'at meals . . . in his chamber a board kept for his chamberlains and the gentlemen ushers, having with them a mess of the young lords and another for gentlemen.'

But however medieval all this may have been, there were important differences between the Tudor noble's place in society and his predecessor's. In the fifteenth century war had presented

50

the noble with opportunities for ransom and for plunder. Many castles were 'partly builded by spoils gotten in France', as Leland said of Sudeley in Gloucestershire; great fortunes were made by nobles like Richard Beauchamp, earl of Warwick; and comfortable nest-eggs amassed by gentlemen like William of Windsor, 'an active and valorous knight rich with great wealth which he had acquired by his martial prowess'. These men responded to opportunity by keeping companies of armed retainers, which, at a time when the crown was impoverished by the battles in France, could menace the stability of State and dynasty. In the sixteenth century such openings were fewer. The estates of the greatest magnates, the dukes of Lancaster and York for instance, had been absorbed by the crown. The foreign wars of the sixteenth century were less frequent and less profitable, and the crown was careful to keep noblemen's retainers more effectively under control. The big families of retainers could still make a lavish show or create a local disturbance, but they could no longer topple thrones or bring riches to their lords. The great fortunes were now to be made, not by war-lords, but by ministers and favourites of the king.

A man of the ministerial type was Sir William Petre. Born into a Devonshire family he studied law at Oxford and entered the royal service. He had two great assets for a political career: a relaxed manner which persuaded others to talk freely to him, and 'a natural gravity, that shut him up' and prevented him from giving himself away. Armed with these qualities he became in turn a visitor of the monasteries, master in chancery, and secretary of state. From the rewards of his service he was able to buy estates of 40,000 acres in Essex and Devon, build the fair-sized manor-house of Ingatestone, and ultimately achieve the honour of entertaining Elizabeth I at his home in 1561. Typical of royal favourites was Robert

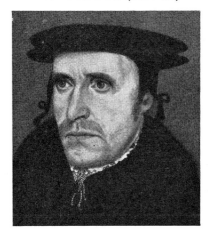

Sir William Petre (1505–72)

51

Dudley, son of the duke of Northumberland and companion of Queen Elizabeth, who created him earl of Leicester in 1564 and lavished on him profitable offices and estates. Such men, whether ministers or favourites, were first and last dependent upon the crown, both for their fortunes and for their survival. The over-mighty subject of Lancastrian days, who could stand against the monarch, was gone, and in his place stood nobles, no less grand, surrounded by no fewer retainers, but looking for advancement to the court. There had of course always been some such men. In the sixteenth century they were dominant. It was not that the Tudors relied upon some mysterious group called a new nobility, but rather that the relationship of the whole nobility, new and old, towards the monarch and society had changed.

'Gentlemen', said Harrison, 'be those whom their race and blood (or at the least their virtues) do make noble and known.' The gentlemen of England were no new class, but they were a growing class, and new riches were spread widely among the

Ingatestone Hall, Essex, begun in 1540: the reward of a political career

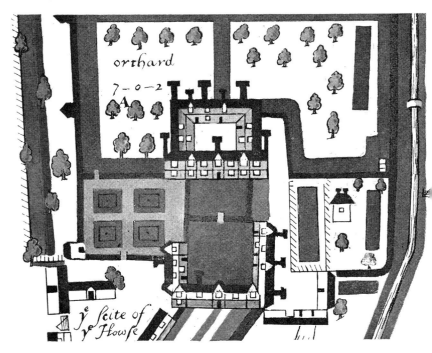

landowners, allowing a degree of pretension and comfort that would have been impossible at the end of the fifteenth century. We shall see something of the comfort in the next chapter. The pretension is illustrated by the search for respectable pedigrees and the elaboration of coats-of-arms. 'Gentility', said the proverb, 'is nothing but ancient riches': all that the *nouveaux riches* needed to achieve gentility was proof that their riches were not new, but old.

The elaboration of coats of arms: the arms on Sir Christopher Hatton tomb, 1593

A coat-of-arms was an essential part of such proof and was therefore widely sought: in 1433 Shropshire held only 48 armigerous families, by 1623 it had 470. The secret of such proliferation lay in the herald's office, a key institution through whose agency a theoretically rigid society could become highly mobile. 'For money', said Sir Thomas Smith, secretary of state, a herald would give a man 'arms newly made and invented, the title whereof shall pretend to have been found by the said herald in perusing and viewing of old registers.' Alternatively the herald could be frank about it and say that the man was worthy to be a gentlemen on account of his virtue or his deeds. In either case the old-established families looked down on the newcomer: 'a great temporal blessing it is', wrote Sir John Wynn of Gwydir in Caernarvonshire, 'and a great heart's ease to a man to find that he is well descended, and a greater grief it is for upstarts and gent of the first head to look back unto their descents, being base in such sort.' But however scornful the older gentry might be, there was nothing that they could do to keep their order a closed caste.

Sir Thomas Gresham (*1519–79*)

Below the gentry in Harrison's social hierarchy came the merchants and the burgesses. The term 'merchant' in Tudor England covered nearly as wide a range of wealth, activity, and respectability as the term 'company director' does today. At the top were rich London businessmen, at the bottom struggling provincial shopkeepers.

The merchant aristocracy of London was a small tight group of men, often related to one another by marriage, dominating the affairs of the city, and, in the case of the greatest, leaving their mark upon national life. One of them, perhaps the most famous of all, was Sir Thomas Gresham. Vastly rich, skilled in finance, subtle and diplomatic, he became the unofficial, though not the unrewarded, economic adviser to all three children of Henry VIII. The story is told of him that, when Elizabeth stayed at his new house at Osterley, she rather rudely announced that the courtyard was too large and would be improved by a wall down the middle. Next morning she found that the wall had been built by labourers despatched at once from London and set to work throughout the night. Gresham had indeed a passion for building. In 1567 he had completed the London Bourse, later christened by Elizabeth the Royal Exchange, and by his will he created Gresham College, intended as a third university. The man who succeeded him as the government's financial adviser and economic ambassador-at-large was Sir Horatio Palavicino, the outstanding member of the small but vigorous group of naturalised foreign merchants. Born into an aristocratic merchant dynasty in Italy, he began his financial career as the Antwerp agent for his family alum business. A political quarrel with the Pope then brought him to England, where he negotiated loans to the Dutch and the French, and ultimately became Elizabeth's ambassador in Germany.

Gresham and Palavicino were national figures, altogether

grander and more influential than most of the London merchants; but the rest made up an impressive enough group.
Members of the great London companies, they were wholesale
traders in every kind of business. They were a small elite,
numbering about 600 at the end of the fifteenth century and 800
a century later, towering above the rest of London's population
and keeping the city government tightly under oligarchic
control. They were highly conscious of their position and did all
they could to advertise it. Their clothes were many, expensive,
and vivid: furs and silks were favourite materials, violet one
of their best-loved colours. They liked their dignity to be
upheld by a good display of servants: a retired tailor once
demanded of his son that when 'I or my wife walketh out, . . .
my said son shall let me have an honest man-child to wait upon
me and an honest maid-child to wait upon my wife, at his own
proper cost'.

Most merchants were of course a great deal
humbler than this in their aspirations. Against
the massive fortunes of the London merchant, the
provincial man could only set estates of half the
size and was content to rule his local roost,
rather than venture into national, or even into
county, politics. Mostly they came from outside
the town in which they traded, having been
apprenticed by their parents to an established
merchant. For instance, the father of Thomas
Prestwood, later of Exeter, 'conceiving a good
hope of him by reason of his pregnant wit and
forwardness, sent him to London', where he
was apprenticed to a rich merchant. Eventually
Prestwood, travelling for his master, met and
married a rich widow of Exeter, set up on his
own in the town, and 'did prosper very well and
increased unto good wealth and riches'. Other
men, of course, were born into trade. One such
was John Johnson, merchant of the Staple in
London, whose father was a Calais trader.
Johnson was apprenticed to Anthony Cave, who

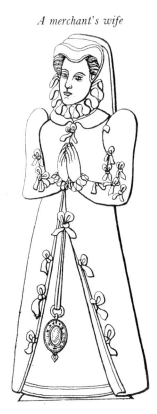

A merchant's wife

55

A London merchant

gave him education and protection: 'I do not forget', wrote Johnson 'that ye have brought me up from my childhood'— though he added that Cave no doubt remembered the faithful service done in return. Johnson sensibly married Cave's niece and his master took him into partnership.

First cousins, so to speak, of the merchants, were the industrialists. Perhaps the best known of all sixteenth-century cloth-manufacturers was William Stumpe, installer of looms and weavers in the empty buildings of Malmesbury Abbey. Stumpe achieved acceptance in county society, became a justice of the peace, member of parliament and sheriff, and founded a landed family, whose social consummation was reached in the marriage of his three great-granddaughters to the earls of Suffolk, Lincoln, and Rutland. He was, of course, exceptional. A more typical clothier might call himself a gentleman, represent his borough in Parliament, and buy himself a country estate. His sons and daughters might ultimately achieve 'county' status. But he himself would not quite belong to the oligarchy of his shire and he ran the risk of being 'disgraded' by the heralds from his self-appointed rank of gentleman.

William Caxton, comparing the merchant families of London with those that he had seen abroad, commented that 'in other lands, in divers cities [merchants] . . . of one name and lineage successively have endured prosperously many heirs', while in London a merchant family 'can unneth [i.e. hardly] continue unto the third heir or scarcely to the second'. He put this down to the inadequacy of the merchants' sons, at whose 'ripening there is no kernel nor good corn found, but chaff for the most part'. Caxton was perhaps unfair in placing the blame upon such shortcomings. One powerful reason for the brief life of commercial dynasties was the conventional disposition of a merchant's estate at death, providing one-third for charity, and dividing the rest between his wife and all his sons. Another was the heavy city mortality, which deprived perhaps 30 per cent of the merchants of a male heir. Possibly most important of all, at least among the leaders of the community, was the traditional urge to set up as a country gentleman. Merchants did not always make the change at once. John Johnson, for instance, having leased the manor house of Glapthorn and built up a flock of over one thousand sheep, continued to find his main occupation in trade. Where Johnson failed to last the full course of transformation—his business went bankrupt in 1553—others succeeded. Thomas Prestwood junior of Exeter, inheriting commercial riches from his father, 'did not much follow the trade of merchandise in which also he was trained up, but lived rather as a gentleman by his lands'. On a much grander scale Horatio Palavicino settled down as a country gentleman, with landed estates of about 8,000 acres and a mansion at Babraham in Cambridgeshire, where he liked to picture himself as a rustic squire 'amongst my shepherds, clipping my sheep'.

Caxton was right in seeing merchant fortunes as ephemeral. Tudor boroughs and cities were great social mixers, importing the sons of gentlemen, shopkeepers, and artisans, exporting successful merchants. They acted as social escalators rather than centres of civilisation, and in consequence many of them now show all the marks of places that people try to leave. Except in London, and possibly in York or Bath, England has never achieved a great urban civilisation comparable with the cities of France, Germany and Italy.

Harrison's description of English society leaves little room for what we should today call 'the professions'. Predictably so, for in the Middle Ages there had been only two occupations which could properly be called professional—the Church and the law—and Harrison was not very responsive to change. Of these two, the clergy were a separate estate and the lawyers, provided they achieved some standing, could count themselves

gentlemen. Some of the other professions that we know today—
medicine and teaching, for instance—were in the hands of the
Church, and others—architecture, surgery, music, and acting—
were held to be the concern of craftsmen or of servants. In
Tudor England some of these occupations were released from
the control of the Church and others began to push upwards into
the higher reaches of society.

It will be easiest to consider doctors, clergymen, school-
masters, dons, and architects (as far as there were any) in the
later chapters on medicine, the Church, education and building.
Here we shall consider three professions: the law, acting and
music. Of these the law was easily the most important. It had a
long and influential history, its leading members were rich
and respected. Throughout the Middle Ages, indeed until the
eighteenth century, legal thinking and practice were of critical
importance in social relationships and in government. Most
men of any standing at all could expect to be involved in
several law suits during their lives—whereas most of us today
regard an appearance in court, for anything more complicated
than a parking offence, as utterly remote. Government was
held to be mainly a matter of administering the law: in conse-

The Court of Wards and Liveries: lawyers in session

quence most government offices were partly law-courts, like the exchequer and the court of wards, and many civil servants had a legal training. Questions of political controversy were often solved, or at least debated, in terms of the law: 'What do the gentlemen of the long robe think?' was a more frequent question than 'What will be the effect of this upon the economy?' In Tudor times the growth of government power and the extending field of its action, coinciding with rapid changes in social and economic structure, gave still greater opportunities for lawyers to achieve riches and power. At the top of the scale some of them, like Sir Edward Coke and Sir Francis Bacon, built up vast fortunes. At the bottom, there was apparently a huge increase in the anonymous mass of country attorneys and their clerks. It is difficult to find out much about such obscure men, but they seem to have become almost a new class by the end of the sixteenth century, a class despised then, but later to grow into the respectable profession of solicitor.

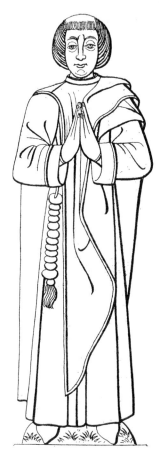

A fifteenth-century lawyer

Not surprisingly this great professional advance was welcomed with a storm of abuse. 'The lawyers they go ruffling in their silks, velvets, and chains of gold: they build gorgeous houses, sumptuous edifices, and stately turrets; they keep a port like mighty potentates. . . . All upon the polling and pilling of the poor commons.' How did they gain their wealth? 'Lawyers . . . getteth their riches rising out of the works of sin and mischief of the common people, for robbing and stealing riches one from another.' They encouraged men to waste their money in litigation, they perverted the law, and they took bribes. Their 'covetous and greedy minds . . . destroyeth all law and good policy.' The lawyers survived these attacks easily enough. Probably they were nothing like so bad personally as their critics supposed. In any case their services were needed by a litigious society, which was happy to pay them while it abused them.

Medieval drama had been elaborate, varied, and complicated. To understand it we have to rid our minds of the current notion of 'the theatre' as a specialised minority resort, for drama in the Middle Ages was essentially a public spectacle. The actors were townsmen performing miracle plays, nobles jousting in the sophisticated display of the tournament, countrymen miming on the village green, and minstrel troupes travelling the roads. Of these only the minstrels were professionals, and they were more like variety artistes than actors. But after the breach with Rome censorship of plays by a government sensitive to religious controversy and repression of wandering vagabonds began to bear sharply on the medieval players. They were forbidden to perform unless they had a royal licence, and such licences were less and less often granted. By Elizabeth's reign English acting was confined to a few small companies based on London, operating by permission of the court, and giving regular performances in public theatres. Within the century the amateur, occasional and provincial drama had been replaced by professional, regular and centralised 'theatre'.

The professionals quickly took the opportunities given to

Amateur players

them by a rich society thirsting for the spectacle and for the drama of which the government's policy had deprived it. But they took these chances only in the face of fierce opposition. Players were maligned as vagabonds, 'light and decayed persons who for filthy lucre are minded . . . to devise and set up in open places shows . . . of unhonest games.' The Puritans attacked them as idle corrupters of the populace, 'crocodiles', 'peevish cattle', 'caterpillars', 'buzzing dronets', 'double-dealing ambodexters', and 'painted sepulchres'. Yet in the end the actors crossed the barriers of social conservatism to establish themselves as a profession—and one of them, William Shakespeare, even called himself a gentleman.

There had been plenty of musicians, professional and amateur, in the Middle Ages. London had its company of musicians, just as it had its tailors, shoemakers, and tanners. It also had its waits, originally night-watchmen, by the sixteenth century primarily musicians,

The Globe theatre, Southwark

appointed to give a musical background to the city's processions. Few other towns had guilds of musicians, but all those with any pretensions at municipal dignity had their waits. Some musicians had posts as servants in noble households, though their number has been greatly exaggerated by legend. Others lived a wandering life, going from town to town, playing where they could. Great cathedrals and colleges had their music-masters and choirs; but these were few, and the average parish church seems to have had little music beyond the congregational singing of the psalms. Above all, there were the musicians of the court. Throughout the Middle Ages English monarchs had had their minstrels for secular occasions and their Chapel Royal, with its chaplains, singing-men, and choir-boys, for ecclesiastical.

Under Henry VIII and Elizabeth the court came to be the leading patron of English music. Edward IV had only five permanent musicians, Edward VI had 65. The Chapel Royal became increasingly specialised and professional. In the fifteenth century all the singing-men were supposed to be 'sufficient in organs playing', and presumably they took turns at it. By 1540 Thomas Tallis had joined the Chapel Royal, and he was followed by William Byrd, William Blitheman, and John Bull, all of them great professional organists. When the standard of performance in many cathedral choirs had declined into what one musician called 'dead-heartedness', it was mainly left to the great musicians of the Chapel Royal, in Thomas Morley's words, 'to draw the hearer in chains of gold by the ears to the consideration of holy things.' Secular music was provided by the men of the King's Musick. They gave dinner-time concerts —'twelve trumpets and two kettle-drums made the hall ring for half-an-hour together', while Elizabeth was eating—and they played at banquets, tournaments, and masques. Many of them, especially under Henry VIII, were Italians, who thus helped to bring England into contact with the revolutionary music of Monteverdi.

The flowering of court music under the Tudors was of enormous importance in English musical history, but was not the only development of the century. The London musicians' guild became alarmed at the competition it encountered from craftsmen and labourers, who, having taken to 'wandering abroad, riot, vice, and idleness, do commonly use nowadays to sing songs called three men's songs in the taverns, alehouses, inns, and such other places of this city'. The Tudor government, always sensitive to the problem of the vagrant poor, always alarmed that wandering minstrels might spread seditious rumours, listened readily to such complaints. Itinerant minstrels were punished as vagabonds unless they were in the service of a noble or a town, and, since the number of musicians in noble households was small, it fell to the town councils to preserve English music in the provinces. Rather surprisingly

Henry VIII as a musician

62

they accepted the task, perhaps because the waits could always be presented as utilitarian watchmen as well as musicians. Thus while music at the centre was increasingly the music of the court, music in the provinces was, by the end of the century, largely municipal.

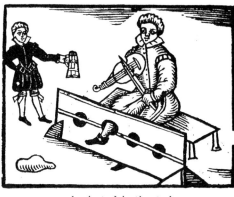

A minstrel in the stocks

Although the singing-men of the Chapel Royal could style themselves gentlemen, professional musicians never seem quite to have attained that status. This may seem surprising when one considers that music was thought an important part of the education of a nobleman. But while members of the upper classes could sing and play they were not expected to display their talents in public. If a gentleman plays 'in a common audience', said Sir Thomas Elyot, it impairs 'his estimation, the people forgetting reverence when they behold him in the similitude of a common servant or minstrel'. It followed from this that anyone who did play publicly could hardly be a gentleman. But if musicians were kept to an inferior status they were at least free from the abuse poured upon lawyers and actors.

Beneath gentry, merchants, and professional men came the yeoman, a term not easily defined, whose meaning was constantly shifting. Legally, as Harrison said, yeomen were those who 'may dispend of their own free land in yearly revenue to the sum of forty shillings sterling'. In practice a man did not need freehold land to make him a yeoman, many of whom held only leasehold or copyhold. Normally they were men who lived by farming, distinguished from the gentry by lesser social pretensions and a readiness to work with their hands, distinguished from the smaller peasantry by their greater wealth. Best known of all sixteenth-century yeomen was Hugh Latimer's father: 'my father was a yeoman, and had no lands of his own, only he had a farm of three or four pound by year at the utter most, and hereupon he tilled so much as kept half-a-dozen men. He had walk for a hundred sheep and my mother milked thirty kine. He was able and did find the king a harness, with himself and his horse. . . . I can remember that I buckled his harness when he went unto Blackheath field.' But now, says Latimer, the man who has the ground is not able to do anything, 'for his prince, for himself, nor for his children, or give a cup of drink to the poor'. This lament has led many people to think that the yeomen of England were going down before the rapacious gentry. But this was certainly not true of them all. The rising price of wool and other produce gave as great an opportunity to the industrious and efficient farmer as it did to the gentry. Many yeoman were indeed richer than some of the gentry:

> *A knight of Wales,*
> *A gentleman of Cales,*
> *A laird of the North Countree,*
> *A yeoman of Kent,*
> *Sitting on his penny rent,*
> *Can buy them out all three.*

Fixed rents, rising prices, and the insatiable market of London were a good basis for prosperity. Piece by piece the yeomen were able to build up their farms.

> *When gentles use walking, with hawks on their hands,*
> *Good husbands with grazing do purchase their lands.*

Tusser's jingle has the ring of truth. It is confirmed by the account of his own family written by Robert Furse of Devonshire. They were, he said, at first men of 'small possession and ability', who had 'by little and little . . . so run their course . . . that by these means we are come to much more possessions, credit, and reputation than ever any of them had'. It was not only from the estates of unthrifty gentlemen that they profited. They were often forward in enclosing land and were sometimes no more scrupulous than the gentry in the means that they employed:

There be many rich men
Both yeomen and gentry
Who for their own private gain
Hurt a whole country.

No doubt there were also many yeomen,
who for one reason or another could not stand
the pace. A ruthless landlord, insecure
tenure, unskilful management, or plain bad
luck might ruin a man. But many, perhaps
most, were pushing ahead, some into the
ranks of the gentry, some content to remain
where they were. Gradually they were beginning to mark out positions of leadership of
their villages. Not every village had its
squire to lord it over the peasants; and in
several of them leadership with all its burdens
was undertaken by the yeoman. He was still,
in the sixteenth century, a peasant and was
long to remain one, but the process was
beginning by which his descendants were
to end, many of them, as gentlemen farmers
or even plain gentlemen.

A prosperous yeoman

What were the special qualities of the yeoman that marked
him off from the gentleman? Essentially he was thrifty and
simple. The gentleman's role was to bear the 'port, charge and
countenance' of his rank, a business that became as time went on
more and more expensive. The yeoman ignored such tempta-
tions. As one yeoman wrote gratefully of his father: 'he was a
man that always loved money well and disposed to great thrift,
and was always careful to increase that portion which he had.'
It might be the epitaph of a class. You could say of them, as
Thomas Fuller did, that 'wise Solon . . . would surely have
pronounced the English yeomanry a fortunate condition', or,
with John Taylor, the water-poet, that

He knows to get, but never knows to give.

It depended on the point of view.

65

A blacksmith in his forge

The last of Harrison's classes contained 'day labourers, poor husbandmen . . . and all artificers'. They were those that 'have neither voice nor authority in the commonwealth', and among them may be counted husbandmen, weavers, domestic servants, bricklayers, landless labourers, and such village craftsmen as the smith and the carpenter. Where in Leicestershire the smaller yeoman might have 80 acres of arable, the husbandman averaged perhaps 30-40, though many had a good deal less than this. He might have ten sheep, half-a-dozen horses, half-a-dozen pigs, a plough, a cart or two, and perhaps three harrows. Like the yeoman he improved his position as the century went on and was certainly living much more comfortably by the end of it. Ranked below the husbandman was the village labourer. In the midlands about one man in every five drew part of his livelihood from wages; but he was seldom wholly dependent upon them, for he would usually have a small holding of five to ten acres as well. Intermediate between these two groups in village society were the craftsmen, of whom the most important was the smith, who also combined his work with a small holding. His occupation was generally hereditary, and the ancestors of Benjamin Franklin were said to have been for generations the smiths of a Northamptonshire village. All these men formed the bottom end of normal village society. They had their peers working at industrial occupations: cloth weavers in the Wiltshire villages, the shearmen of Shrewsbury who 'finished' the woven cloth, the tin-miners of Cornwall, and the building labourers in every town. But there is no space to talk of these diverse crafts, whose practitioners in any case left few traces of their lives.

One thing they all had in common was insecurity. Very often they might prosper, but for much of the time they lived on the edge of subsistence, in danger of being thrown by any accident into the great army of the destitute. Neither poverty nor insecurity were new arrivals in Tudor England, but the poor, as a social class, were. Horrifying as the scourges of medieval life seem today, men and women had at least a secure place in society and on the land. The old and the infirm could expect care within the manor. A system which tied men to the land also ensured that most of them had a plot, however small, for sustenance. The changes in the economy from the Black Death onwards removed these social props and sent into the world a mass of men with no land, no social roots, no security. Thomas More described the peasants who were compelled to sell their lands: 'they must needs depart away, poor, silly, wretched souls, men, women, husbands, wives, fatherless children, widows, woeful mothers, with their young babes. . . . Away they trudge . . . finding no place to rest in'. When they have reached the end of their tether 'what can they then else do but steal, and justly pardy be hanged, or else go about begging?'

The dispossessed peasantry flocked into the towns looking for work, and brought there the new problem of urban poverty. The critical point of social need came in the towns and the clothing districts: here poverty was at its worst, here the most striking efforts were made at controlling it. The cloth industry gave the best opportunity of employment, and its growth in the 1530s and 1540s enabled it to absorb many of the poor. But the cloth trade was notoriously unstable and the slump of 1551 was only the first of many. Rising population flooded the labour market, depressed wages, and brought unemployment.

Vagabonds

To contemporaries the most urgent problem of all was vagrancy. There were said to be perhaps 10,000 homeless vagrants, men, women, and children, wandering over the countryside, breeding, begging, and stealing. Their lives seemed so shocking and sinful that one writer exploded against 'the abominable, wicked, and detestable debauch of . . . these ragged rabblement of rakehells, that under the pretence of great misery . . . do win great alms'. Begging developed, during the middle of the sixteenth century, almost into a profession, with its apprenticeship, initiation ceremonies, and specialised branches. Ruling over all was the 'upright-man', said to be of 'great authority', since 'all sorts of beggars are obedient to his hests'. Beneath his rule were such frauds as the counterfeit cranks, who pretended to be stricken with the falling sickness, the Abraham men, who pretended to be mad, and the dommerers, who pretended to be deaf mutes. Rather superior to beggars were confidence tricksters, sometimes called conny-catchers. While the beggars were the product of the new poverty, the conny-catchers were rather the product of the new riches, since their trade was to strip the rich and foolish of their money, which they did by card-sharping, the use of loaded dice and so on.

To the respectable landowners and merchants this growing army of poor presented a problem as new, shocking and intract-

Whipping vagrants through the streets

able as the industrial proletariat of the factory age or the urban African of modern Johannesburg. Uncomprehending and frightened, the ruling classes reacted with the savagery later to be shown by nineteenth-century businessmen and twentieth-century 'whites'. Branding, whipping, and deportation were all proposed. Even so, as time went by, under the influence of new religious impulses, the attitudes softened and there began a remarkable flow of charity, which we shall discuss in a later chapter.

An Abraham man

Harrison says nothing of one great social gulf, the difference in status between men and women. But luckily Sir Thomas Smith, the secretary of state, who plagiarised Harrison's description of the degrees of society, here branches out on his own. Of the two sexes, each, said Smith, had his own function: 'the man to get, to travail abroad, to defend'; the wife 'to save that which is gotten, to tarry at home, . . . to keep all at home neat and clean'. Each had qualities fit for the task: 'the man stern, strong, bold, adventurous, negligent of his beauty, and spending'; 'the woman weak, fearful, fair, curious of her beauty, and saving'. That the man in the sixteenth-century household was the spender we can readily believe, that he was negligent of his beauty is harder to accept in front of the jewelled hats, ruffs, and capes that parade in Tudor portraits.

Smith's belief in the inferiority of women stemmed in part from St Paul's version of Christianity: 'he that is unmarried careth for the things that belong to the Lord, how he may please the Lord; but he that is married careth for the things that are of the world, how he may please his wife'. St Chrysostom put the point less ponderously: woman is a 'necessary evil, a natural temptation, a desirable calamity, a domestic peril, a deadly fascination, and a painted ill'. The duty of woman was,

Countryman and his wife

in essence, to 'learn in silence with all subjection'. This Oriental view of women inherent in Christianity was reinforced by the structure of a feudal society, organised for fighting. In such a society man was bound to be uppermost. 'The wife', said some medieval judges, 'in her husband's lifetime has nothing of her own nor can she make any purchase with her own money.' According to medieval lawyers, she was 'under the rod' of her husband.

This medieval attitude to women still prevailed in the Tudor period and beyond. The legal status of a wife was best summed up by a seventeenth-century lawyer. 'If a seignoress of a manor marry her bondman, he is made free, and where before he was her footstool, he is now her head and seignor.' A man could, without fear of legal redress, beat 'an outlaw, a traitor, a pagan, his villein, or his wife'. A woman stood to suffer sharp punishments for offending against her husband, even up to the penalty of being burned alive for murdering him. The great danger in male minds was equality. 'Where the woman stands upon terms of equality with her husband . . . the very root of all good carriage is quite withered, and the fountain thereof utterly dried up.'

Such was the voice of the law and of the Church. But there were changes in the sixteenth century. In place of the traditional Catholic attitude that marriage was a necessary evil for those too weak to continue in the higher state of virginity, Protestants preached that marriage was the natural state. They attacked the Pope on the ground that 'the most holy state of godly matrimony hath he most vilely and most wickedly enbased, cast down, and made almost of no reputation'. Although they emphasised the wife's duty of obedience, English Puritans said

70

that 'the subjection we treat of is not slavish, but equal and royal in a sort'.

Women themselves were taking advantage of the neo-Platonic attitude to their sex which had become dominant in Italy. The great emphasis upon learning, the belief that women should be the intellectual companions of men, and the example of noblewomen like Isabella d'Este Gonzaga spread north to England. Among the first to urge these views was Sir Thomas More, whose daughter, Margaret, translated one of the works of Erasmus. One of the greatest to benefit from them was Queen Elizabeth, whose tutor, Roger Ascham, wrote of her: 'her mind has no womanly weakness, her perseverance is equal to that of a man, and her memory long keeps what it quickly picks up.' But even in complimenting her, he revealed a certain contempt for her sex.

These changes bewildered men. Some, in reaction, urged that women should be kept in their places; others that they should be freed. All joined in the prolonged controversies of the sixteenth

Sir Thomas More and his family

A noblewoman

and seventeenth centuries about the nature of women, controversies whose nature can best, or least tediously, be summarised by the titles of some of the pamphlets produced: *The Schole House of Women*; *The prayse of all Women*; *A dyalogue defensive for women agaynst malycyous detractoures*; *The Arraignment of Lewd, Idle, Froward and unconstant women*; and so on. There were no such controversies about the nature of men, and that in itself shows that society was still dominated by males. But they were very worried males, concerned that a subordinate section of society might be getting out of hand. Their endless discussion of the nature of women reminds one irresistibly of the equally endless discussions today about the adolescent. The parallel is obvious.

Foreigners, however, seem to have thought Englishwomen lucky and charming. 'England is a paradise for women, a prison for servants, and a hell for horses', went a foreign proverb. It was true that 'the women there are entirely in the power of their

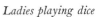

Ladies playing dice

husbands except for their lives', yet they were not 'shut up but they have the free management of the house or housekeeping', which they were able to leave to servants, so that they could spend the day in riding, playing cards, or gossiping. Less sophisticated than continental women, they were seen to have a

72

freshness and a natural beauty: 'the women there are charming and by nature so mighty pretty as I have scarcely ever beheld, for they do not falsify, paint, or bedaub themselves as in Italy and other places; but they are somewhat awkward in their style of dress.' Erasmus, a susceptible scholar, was captivated by their habit of kissing: 'wherever you go,' he wrote, 'everyone welcomes you with a kiss, and the same on bidding farewell. . . . If you were once to taste them, and find how delicate and fragrant they are, you would certainly desire . . . till death to be a sojourner in England.'

The degrees of society were mirrored in its clothes. 'As for their outward show,' said Sir Thomas Smith, 'a gentlemen . . . must go like a gentleman, a yeoman like a yeoman, and a rascal like a rascal.'

Fifteenth-century dress: a fur-lined gown

The tight, padded doublets, and high, starched ruffs of the Elizabethan age could certainly not be worn by anyone with a job of work to be done. Nor could anyone but the rich have afforded materials at 10s. 8d. a yard or a damask gown at £81, at a time when a clergyman's stipend could be less than £10 per annum. The clothes of the lower ranks of society were not untouched by high fashion, but they were simpler, looser, and more conservative: merchants continued to wear the long loose-fitting gown for decades after its abandonment by the nobility.

In the time of Henry VIII it is the male dress that strikes one, as indeed it was meant to do (see Frontispiece). Men's costume was made up of several layers of loose garments, shirt, doublet, jerkin, and gown, on the upper half of the body, with stockings, or hose, on the legs. The silhouette presented was thus massive and thrusting, with a bulky torso carried upon legs that were freed for movement. The impact of this virility was emphasised by the use of the codpiece, and the grandeur of the wearer was displayed by the

73

slashings of the doublet and the puffing of the sleeves. Women's costume was almost dowdy by comparison with this. The upper part of the body was tightly moulded by the gown, which then flared out into the loose and flowing skirt. Fairly ample decolletage gave some opportunity for the use of jewellery, but the total effect was demure and restrained.

From about the middle of the century the dress of both sexes changed. Men abandoned their free and strikingly male silhouette for clothes that were more restricting and, in a way, more 'feminine'. The doublet was padded to resemble a sort of close-fitting armour; waists were pinched in and emphasised by the highly decorated stomacher; and the neck was hidden by the tall starched ruff. Female clothes made a break-through in fashion by the use of separate bodice and skirt. In place of the flowing skirt of the early part of the century, women now wore farthingales—hoops of wire—beneath the skirt to push it out into more rigid shapes. Both sexes loaded themselves with jewellery and set off their clothes with slashing, embroidery, and lace.

Sir Walter Raleigh: the 'feminine' mode

Not that every man in the landed class devotedly followed the fashions. For instance, Sir Richard Bulkeley of Beaumaris wore round breeches and thick bombast doublets whatever the current mode, on the sensible ground that people changed their tastes so often 'that once in every seven years they would turn to his fashion.' Bulkeley's conservatism points the moral. For this was an age when men's

74

clothes as well as women's were constantly changing in order that their wearers could claim to be 'in the fashion'. In our own day male costume changes by shifts of line and cut perceptible only to the *cognoscenti*, and its principal feature is neatness and discretion. Except in one section of our society: male adolescents are constantly developing new fantasies of dress and imposing new tests to distinguish 'in' from 'out'. They provide a bizarre parallel to the

Elizabeth I, bedecked with jewels

gentry of Tudor England, who, also enjoying new wealth, spent it on the status symbols of fashion and wore their clothes with the same assertive air.

The belief in a fixed order and the realities of social change were ever in conflict. However firmly men might believe that the classes were clearly marked off from one another and that the orders of society were built into a divinely ordained pyramid, human conduct contradicted their assumption. It was quite possible for men to move from one class to another, for the nobility and the gentry to engage in the enterprises of trade, for merchants to copy the manners and pretensions of land-owners. New classes, or rather new professions, were thrusting into public notice and demanding recognition. Deeply disturbing as this was, it led men, not to drop the social theories which were thus being undermined, but to reassert them with the aggressive vigour of uncertainty.

Further Reading

W. Harrison. *Description of England* (ed. F. J. Furnivall), 1877
J. H. Hexter, *Reappraisals in History*, 1961: Chapters 2, 4, 5, 6
F. G. Emmison, *Tudor Secretary; Sir William Petre at Court and Home*, 1961
Barbara Winchester, *Tudor Family Portrait*, 1955
W. L. Woodfill, *Musicians in English Society*, 1953
M. C. Bradbrook, *The Rise of the Common Player*, 1962
W. G. Hoskins, *The Midland Peasant*, 1957
M. Campbell, *The English Yeoman*, 1942
Doris Stenton, *The English Woman in History*, 1957

Fool with a mirror: a satire on fashions

IV

Castles, Palaces and Houses

In almost every age men have raised buildings that dominate the landscape, catch the eye and proclaim the beliefs and preoccupations of their founders. The Egyptians displayed their ideals in tombs, the Romans in triumphal arches. Englishmen have lavished money on castles, cathedrals, and monasteries in the Middle Ages, on factories, churches, and railway stations in the nineteenth century, on cinemas in the reign of George V, and on officeblocks in the reign of Elizabeth II. Under the Tudors far and away the most impressive buildings to go up were the palaces of kings and nobles—just as monasteries were the most impressive buildings to come down.

Like clothes, the buildings of the day became ever more bold and assertive:

> *Building royally*
> *Their mansions curiously,*
> *With turrets and with towers,*
> *With halls and with bowers,*
> *Stretching to the stars . . .*

Skelton's attack on Cardinal Wolsey was prophetic of the century. First the kings, then nobles, gentry, and finally yeomen were caught by the urge to build—and to build for show. 'If ever curious building did flourish in England', said Harrison, 'it is in these our years, wherein our workmen excel.'

Henry VII began the craze with Richmond Palace at Sheen,

77

Richmond Palace, Surrey, completed by Henry VII in 1501

Wolsey continued it with Hampton Court, and Henry VIII, 'the only phoenix of his time for fine and curious masonry', brought it to a royal climax with the fantastic elaborations of Nonsuch. Before the accession of the Tudors, English monarchs were badly off for palaces, and few of those that they had were very impressive. The burning of Richmond Palace in 1499 presented Henry VII with the opportunity to make a new beginning and he gave outward expression to the grandeur of his Court in the tall and slender brick towers that now rose above the Thames. Continuing the fashion, his son's chief minister, Cardinal Wolsey, began to build Hampton Court in 1515 and gave it to the king in 1525. The plan of this palace furnished a blue-print for Henry's own building later. It was based upon two courtyards, an outer with a dominating gate-house and the lesser rooms, an inner with the royal lodgings, the chapel, and the great hall. But apart from this basic element of design Hampton Court was aesthetically confused. 'As for the rooms,' said a foreign visitor, 'there is no imaginable order, as the English merely look to convenience.'

This could hardly be said of Henry VIII's greatest palace, the wonder of sixteenth-century England, Nonsuch Palace, near Ewell in Surrey. In 1538 Henry destroyed the church and village of Cuddington, building on their site a palace that took nine

78

years to finish and cost at least £24,000, a colossal sum by the standards of the day. Its plan was based upon the inner and outer courtyards of Hampton Court, each entered through a large and fortified gatehouse. The outer court, facing towards the north, presented an austere and castellated face to the world. The inner court, however, was described as a 'fair and very curious structure', with its upper storey 'richly adorned'. Here Henry built for show, competing with the lush renaissance masterpieces of Europe, like Francis I's chateau at Chambord. The feel of the place is best caught by Hofnaegel's well-known view from the south. Hiding the lower part of the palace is the wall of the privy garden, but above it rises the ornate south front, dominated by the great octagonal towers at each end, with the southern face of the inner gatehouse in the centre. The contrast between that face and the castellated northern front suggests more clearly than anything else the two styles of this extraordinary building, medieval fortification and renaissance display.

This contrast between defensiveness and display also marks the history of private building. In the early Middle Ages great magnates had lived in castles built for war, whose demands

Nonsuch Palace, Surrey, begun in 1538: the ornate south front

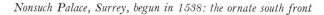

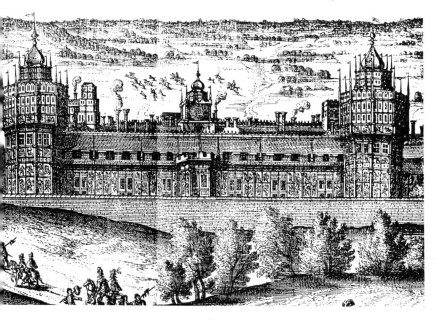

overrode the claims of comfort or of beauty. Lesser men, unable to afford castles, had built fortified manors, like Stokesay, which were residences before they were forts. By the fifteenth century this fashion began to spread upwards, for warfare no longer reached its climax in the siege of baronial castles. The castle became a barracks rather than a strong-point, and with the needs of defence less paramount, comfort and beauty could be better considered. To what effect can be seen at Oxburgh Hall in Norfolk, whose large and beautiful traceried windows gave light and air to those within. Such flimsy structures would have been disastrous in a siege.

The culmination of this development, indeed its finale, came at Thornbury Castle in Gloucestershire, begun by the duke of Buckingham in 1511. A large outer courtyard on the west was used for housing the one or two hundred retainers normally to be found there. An imposing and defensible gatehouse led from this court into the inner quadrant, which housed on the east side the chapel and the hall, on the south the 'stately lodgings' of the duke and the duchess, with great oriel windows looking onto the privy garden. Thus at Thornbury a great magnate combined the sinews of power with the contemporary fashion

Thornbury Castle, Gloucestershire, begun in 1511, with its fine oriel windows

Cowdray, Sussex: the interior of the great court

for comfort and display. Or rather, he began to do so, for in 1521, with his castle still unfinished, the duke was executed on a charge of treason. The pretensions of Thornbury give some slight ground for Henry's jealousy.

With Buckingham's death the building of private castles came to an end. True, some Tudor houses looked like castles, but their turrets were only a sort of stage scenery. For, violent though life still was, power rested now on influence at court, not on mercenary armies, and neither barracks nor fortifications were any longer needed. The best comment on the new age was made in stone by the tough and power-loving Sir John Perrott, when he pierced the outer walls of Carew Castle in Pembrokeshire with large, indefensible mullioned windows.

Having surrendered their defensive walls, the houses of the great did not at once turn welcoming faces to the world. In the early sixteenth century they were still turned in upon themselves, with symmetry and decoration inside the courtyard, their outer walls bare and austere. At Cowdray in Sussex, for instance, beauty was intended only for those who entered, not for all. The ranges of this courtyard house look, from the outside, rambling and ill-designed; only the gatehouse shows any attempt at proportion. But once inside the court, the visitor is surrounded by symmetry and grace.

81

Gradually there were changes in outlook and style. By the reign of Elizabeth the great houses of the land showed an entirely different air, looking out upon the world to display the grandeur and taste of their owners. Such houses were meant to impress, and to impress with a purpose; they were built to accommodate the queen and her court. Sir Christopher Hatton showed his intention when he announced that he would not so much as look at his new house at Kirby until 'that holy saint'

Longleat, Wiltshire, 1547–80: the high renaissance in England

—he meant Queen Elizabeth—'might sit in it'. To achieve their ends Hatton and men like him paid homage to continental tastes, reflecting the interest of their class in the learning and arts of Italy, Flanders, and France. They included classical details in the design, above all they attempted to present a symmetrical façade. These aims were very well achieved at Longleat. Built around a traditional courtyard, so that it should be large enough for the court, Longleat, with its large

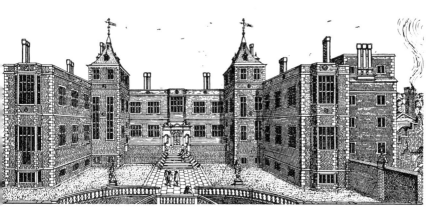

Wimbledon, Surrey, begun 1588: a prodigy house

windows and symmetrical façades, is essentially outward-looking. But it had no successors and remains the only Tudor house built entirely in the high renaissance style. The other great buildings of the later Tudor period owed something to classical form, and more to classical decoration, but their owners had a taste for exuberant display which demanded an effect more striking than classical restraint and balance. That effect can be seen in the tall pinnacles and turrets of Worksop Manor and the bold projections of Wimbledon House. These buildings were designed to present an image of grandeur and they had to be large enough for the Queen and the court. From these demands emerged the characteristic half-H plan of Elizabethan and Jacobean prodigy-houses. This plan allowed a long gallery, a hall, and a great chamber—all the trappings of a

Worksop Manor, Nottinghamshire, built before 1590, probably by Robert Smythson

court; provided them at less cost than the courtyard house; and gave scope for the manipulation of wings and towers to the greatest effect. Such were the considerations that formed the great English house of the day, classical in ornament and symmetry, Gothic in its towers and pinnacles.

The prodigy-houses of the Tudor period were not very many; they hardly could be. Most of the gentry did not aspire to entertain the monarch, nor did they wish to project so costly and exuberant an image of themselves. They were content with houses that aimed at a classical symmetry, but owed much more to native tradition, that seem now to fit the landscape in a way that the prodigy-houses do not. England is covered with them: Barrington Court in Somerset, Loseley in Surrey, Snitterton Hall in Derbyshire, Whitehall in Shrewsbury, and scores of others. They are solid and modest buildings with plain, undecorated exteriors. But this external simplicity is not matched within. Harrison speaks of the 'abundance of arras, rich hangings of tapestry, silver vessel, and so much other plate as may furnish sundry cupboards'. Walls were hung with tapestry or wainscotted in oak. The linenfold panelling of the early Tudor period was replaced as time went by with more

Barrington Court, Somerset, built before 1530: an early Tudor manor house

elaborate designs. Ceilings, which once had beams and joists exposed, were now plastered over with rich and complex patterns. Where the fire-place had once been set in a plain rectangular space, vaster and ever more decorated chimney-pieces now reared up to dominate the rooms.

To many people the term 'Tudor' brings a vision of black-and-white town houses rather than the stone or brick country houses that I have been describing. In fact, since the genuine Tudor houses of most towns have disappeared, the 'black-and-white' is usually either Jacobean or Victorian. In London, for instance, fire

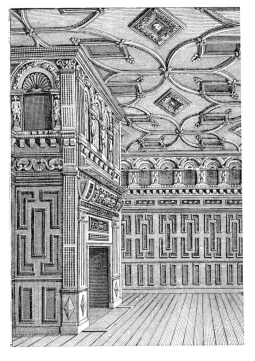

Chimney-piece, panelling and ceiling of c. 1545

and rising site values have left no timber-framed buildings of the sixteenth century intact. But there are some places— towns like Chester, Exeter, and Shrewsbury, which were rich in Tudor times but have since stood still—where genuine half-timbered houses can still be found. These houses were built to a plan, called the unit-house, dictated by the space available, in particular by the competition for street frontage. Each house lay at right-angles to the street, with a shop on the ground-floor front, kitchen and service rooms behind. On the first floor was the hall or living-room running back from the street; and on the second, third, and perhaps fourth floors were the bedrooms. This kind of house was often built to a fair height with over-sails hanging out above the street. Even so this did not satisfy the ambitions of the richer Elizabethan merchants, who put several of these unit-houses together in a double, or even a triple, front. Love of display could then be satisfied by wood-

85

carving that grew ever more elaborate as the century went on.

But these were the houses of prosperous men in important commercial centres. In a smaller market town like Leicester something very much humbler would be found. Here very few houses were more than two storeys high and the carving was much plainer. These smaller town houses resembled the dwellings of lesser men—yeomen, husbandmen, cottagers—in country districts. These varied a good deal from one region to another. In Kent a typical yeoman's house at the beginning of the century might have a hall, with two downstairs bedrooms at one end of it and service rooms at the other. Probably the bedrooms would have a loft above them, while the hall would be open to the roof. A characteristic style of Kentish building was the 'wealden' house with its hall set back, two wings pushed forward, and the upper storey jettied out to form a canopy over the front of the hall. Further north and west such elaboration was rare and houses with only one room were common. In Cornwall, according to the local historian of the time, Richard Carew, husbandmen lived in houses 'with walls of earth, low thatched roofs, few partitions, no planchings or

A typical wealden house: Brewer St Farm, Bletchingley, Kent

glass windows, and scarcely any chimneys, other than a hole in the wall to let out the smoke'.

In Wales, Cumberland, and Devonshire a different type of house was to be found: the long-house, which sheltered both men and animals. At one end of it was the byre for cows, and at the other, raised a little above it, the family dwelling. Between the two ran a cross-passage or feeding walk, from which the living-rooms and the cattle-shed could be entered. An extract from the fourteenth-century Mabinogion describes one of the most primitive of these arrangements: 'on entering, they found the floor uneven and full of puddles, and where it sloped it was difficult to stand thereon, so slippery was it with the mire of cattle. And where

Half-timbered house at Chester

the puddles were, a man might go up to his ankles in water and the urine of cattle.' To judge from a hostile pamphlet called *Wallography*, houses in Wales had not much changed by the seventeenth century: 'every edifice being a Noah's Ark, where a promiscuous family, a miscellaneous heap of all kind of creatures did converse together in one room.'

As the sixteenth century drew on, more abundant riches and the craze for building began to move down the social scale. Yeomen put up new houses or improved old ones. In Kent the halls were given ceilings, so that extra rooms or lofts were provided above—though most people in those days still preferred to sleep downstairs. Since boarding over the hall prevented the smoke from escaping through a hole in the roof,

Ornamental brick chimneys

chimneys had to be built, and these, as the outward signs of internal improvement, were intricately patterned to fulfil their role as status symbols, forerunners of the television aerials of our own day. Harrison commented that the old men of his time were amazed at 'the multitude of chimneys lately erected, whereas in their young days there were not above two or three, if so many, in most uplandish towns of the realm'. The west and the north still lagged behind, but began slowly to follow the lead given by the south-east. Even in Cornwall, according to Carew, the 'husbandman conformeth himself with a better supplied civility to the eastern pattern'. In the Devonshire long-house living quarters came to be separated from the animals' byre by something more substantial than the open cross-walk, and chimneys were built boldly in front of the houses for all to see.

The contents and furnishings of such houses matched the improvements in design. Pillows, once thought fit only for women in childbirth, were now common. Pewter plates and spoons took the place of wooden. Windows were almost always made of glass: horn was never used by the end of the century, lattices seldom. Yet glass was still so expensive that when the earl of Northumberland was not in residence at Alnwick Castle, it was taken out of the windows 'because through extreme winds the glass of the windows of this and other of my lord's castles and houses here in the country doth decay and waste'. If even an earl had to treat glass with such care, it must have seemed precious indeed to a yeoman.

In spite of these advances, the household goods of a yeoman were austere enough by modern standards. Alexander Paramore was a Kentish farmer with 25 acres of arable land, 16 cattle,

88

six horses, 114 sheep, and 14 pigs. His house contained a hall with a kitchen at one end and two bedrooms at the other. Above the bedrooms was a loft. In the hall, which was decorated with a painted cloth, the family dined, Paramore seated on a chair, the others on a bench round the table. They ate off pewter dishes with tin spoons. Some cooking was done on the hall fire, the rest in the kitchen. Two kettles, two iron pans, three brass pots, two spits, and a dripping pan made up the kitchen equipment; and there were also brewing implements and dairy vessels. The better bedroom had two feather beds and two linen-chests, the other a single flock bed. The second bedroom seems also to have acted as an overflow storeroom—a situation familiar to some of us today: in it were two spinning-wheels, a flour bin, two tubs and two chests. In the loft above were two more beds. The house was lit at night by three pewter candlesticks. Simple as Paramore's goods may have been they were luxurious compared with the establishment of John Symons of Derbyshire, a well-to-do man by local standards. Symons had only bedding, two coffers, a trestle table, pewter worth 3s. 8d., a posnet, a spit, two pots, and two pans.

Building materials, like the houses themselves, varied from one region to another. Up to the beginning of the Tudor era most houses, except the largest and the smallest, were timber-framed, especially in the south-east and the west, where wood was plentiful. The simplest kind of timber-framed house was based on the 'cruck'. A tree with a strong outgrow-ing branch would be cut down, the smaller branches lopped off, and the remaining angled timber sliced down the

An early Tudor kitchen

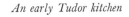

A cruck frame

middle into two identical pieces. The two halves were then joined together at the top to form an inverted 'u', known as a pair of crucks. A similar pair was placed at the other end of the site and the ridge rafter rested between them. Wall and roof were thus continuous, and the head-room within was limited. More elaborate and more expensive was the box-frame in two parts: upon a rectangular base rested the triangular roof, whose ridge-piece and rafters were held up by king-posts and purlins, resting on the walls and tie-beams. The spaces between the main beams of the walls would then be filled with smaller pieces of timber, known as studs, and the gaps between them with flint or brick or, most likely, wattle-and-daub. Wattles were upright stakes through which thin pliant branches were woven; and on this lattice-work foundation would be daubed earth or clay or plaster, bound together with hair or straw. The timber rafters of the roof would normally be covered with thatch, slates, or tiles.

The box frame: Tudor house at Somersham, Suffolk

In western shires the wattle-and-daub was then white-washed and the timbers coated with tar to preserve them against the weather. This produced the familiar black-and-white effect of these houses. So easily does this effect recall the past that some people even whitewash their bricks and then paint in black beams to produce the illusion of antiquity. Rather pleasanter and less easily imitated were the houses of the south-east, where the wood was

Half-timbered cottages in 1558, from a contemporary map by Wyngaerde

left in its natural state and the pale, mellow colour of the frame tones better with the unpainted brick.

Owners of the very smallest houses often could not afford timber-framing. In Devon many cottages were built of cob, a material made by mixing wet earth with lime and straw. Even in the seventeenth century, according to Richard Symonds, 'ordinary houses are of soil mingled with straw, without posts'. Given a solid plinth on which to rest and a good roof to protect them from the rain, cob houses are durable and warm. With their walls painted white, yellow or pink they are, as tourists in the south-west know, gay and attractive as well.

Stone had long been the principal material for castles, monasteries, and churches. In the fifteenth and sixteenth centuries it came increasingly to be used for medium-sized houses too. It was of course especially favoured in districts which had little wood of their own or else had quarries of building stone—in Cornwall, for instance, and above all in the limestone belt which runs north-east across England from Portland Bill through the Cotswolds to Lincolnshire. The range of English limestone is immense, taking in hard, white 'urban' Portland and the mellow golden stone of the Cotswolds. Where the local stone has been used for building in a district, the harmony of house and landscape is at once apparent. Houses like Cothele in Cornwall or Barrington Court in Somerset show how middling country houses were being built in stone at the beginning of our period. But it was not until the seventeenth century that stone acquired its social cachet and began to replace timber in the houses of the well-to-do. During the Tudor epoch timber mansions were still common and merchants in towns like Shrewsbury found elaborately carved wood a better status symbol than stone.

Nowadays we expect houses to be made of brick. But although bricks had been widely used by the Romans, they were neither made nor used in England during the Middle Ages. Only in the fifteenth century did they once more become common, and they were then used only in large structures like Eton College and Hurstmonceux Castle. Under the Tudors brick was much commoner, but often as decoration rather than the principal material of the fabric. Until the cost of brick-making fell in the late seventeenth century, it was still a rare and specialised medium for the rich alone.

Early brick building: Eton college

Who were the architects of Tudor England? In the modern sense of the word there were none. Medieval buildings had been put up by master-craftsmen —masons and carpenters—to a design agreed with their employer. Since most large buildings were of stone, the master-mason's control of his craft gave him the dominating influence over design and a role not far removed from that of the modern architect. He maintained this influence throughout the sixteenth century in the construction of smaller country houses, while the master-carpenter generally directed operations in the building of timber-framed farm-houses. At

92

Patron and master-mason directing operations

the top end of the social scale the Crown also continued to conduct its building in the traditional manner. Control was vested in the Office of Works, under its Surveyor-General, who was usually a craftsman. He and his colleagues—the master-mason, the master-carpenter, the serjeant plumber, and others—were responsible for the building of Henry VIII's great palaces, and it is often possible to discover the man who designed a particular building or feature. For instance, James Needham, surveyor from 1532 to 1546, was the carpenter who designed the great hammer-beam roof at Hampton Court, while his colleague John Molton, master-mason from 1528 until 1547, built the hall itself. These men were in the tradition of Henry Yvele and William Wynford. Like modern architects they were responsible for the plan; unlike modern architects they were also craftsmen in wood or stone.

In the range of building between the royal palace on the one hand and the small manor-house on the other, there came a break with medieval tradition. The fashionable courtier had to show that he was *au fait* with continental tastes; he had to incorporate renaissance details into his house—strap-work, grotesques, and so on; more important still, he had to create a symmetrical and dramatic façade. Such things were rather beyond the ken of native craftsmen, and thus the master-mason was gradually relegated by shifts of style to a lesser role. Greater responsibility then rested upon the employer for explaining what he wanted, and in the course of the century various books were written to help him do so. One of the most interesting of these was John Shute's *First and Chief Groundes of*

Architecture, the earliest architectural treatise printed in England. Shute, who called himself a painter and an architect, was sent to Italy in 1550 by his patron, the duke of Northumberland, to study buildings. Essentially he was a theorist rather than a craftsman, and a highly academic theorist at that. For he thought that the architect should be acquainted with grammar, geometry, arithmetic, philosophy, optics, physics, and music—and be 'not altogether ignorant in astronomy'. He need not, one is relieved to know, be perfect in all of these, but he must learn something of each. Shute's practical advice was clearly derived from Italian treatises. He noticed the close connection emphasised by Italians between the proportions of the human body and the proportions of a building, and he introduced these proportions into his descriptions of the various orders of architecture—the Tuscan, for instance, was to be 'made upon the symmetry of a strong man'. As will by now be obvious, Shute was the forerunner less of the architect than of the architectural critic. Rather more practical in his advice was Andrew Boorde, doctor of physic, author of *The Boke for to lerne a man to be wyse in buylding of his howse*. Houses, he said, should be built in country that was well watered and well-wooded. The air must be clean, for foul air 'doth putrify the brain and doth corrupt the heart'. Builders must be especially careful in siting the latrines: 'permit no common pissing house to be about the house or mansion, and let the common house of

The Tuscan order: the symmetry of a strong man

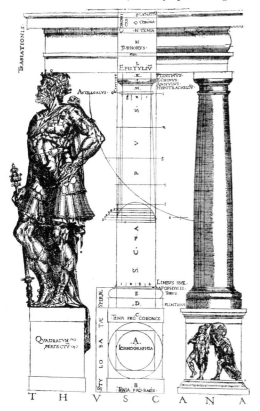

94

easement be over some water, or else elongated from the house.'

Neither Shute nor Boorde was a leader of opinion; and new artistic ideas were brought into mid-sixteenth-century England, not by them, but by the politicians and civil servants who followed Edward Seymour, duke of Somerset, Protector of the Realm.

Masons at work

Seymour himself used French classical models for Somerset House in the Strand. Sir Thomas Smith, his secretary of state, owned five copies of the Roman treatise on architecture by Vitruvius. Sir William Sharington, a shady political adventurer who performed various frauds at the mint, was behind much of the work at Thomas Seymour's Sudeley Castle, the duke of Northumberland's Dudley Castle, and his own Lacock Abbey.

Another member of this circle was William Cecil, who began in 1556 to rebuild his family house at Burghley, near Stamford. His part in the work shows just how much the owner had to be the chief designer too. At the very start Roger Ward, the master-mason on the spot, wrote to Cecil for detailed instructions: what was to be the design of the dormer windows in the inner court? what did Cecil intend for the stairs of the base court? If Cecil would 'draw your meaning how and after what fashion you would have them to be made in all points', then Ward would do his best. Five years later Cecil was dealing through a general estate factotum, Peter Kemp, who was sending him detailed suggestions about some of the rooms. One of his principal concerns was to avoid having the house's water supply contaminated by the stable. To this end he sent a plan for running the water to the top of the house and letting it run down again, but he apologised for his sketch, 'the manner thereof it is not very sightly for that I am not cunning in drawing'. In 1564 Cecil consulted yet another kind of expert, Edmund Hall, a surveyor, and two years after that he employed a Flemish mason to design pillars for a gallery. Two things stand out from this story: there was no single plan for the house before building started; and the man responsible for planning the details and the whole was Cecil himself.

Courtiers who wished to build could always get help from surveyors, men skilled in many of the complicated tasks of estate management. The most famous of such men in the second half of the century was John Thorpe, son of a mason, clerk in the Office of Works, and a busy land surveyor. Thorpe left behind him a fascinating collection of designs, and it is tempting to see in such a man the successor to the medieval mason and the precursor of the modern architect. Tempting, but largely false. For while the surveyor might advise, he had none of the mason's technical skill. Nor had he the responsibility of the architect: in the words of a seventeenth-century owner-builder the surveyor's task was to 'survey and direct the building to the form I conceived and plotted it'. Responsibility and leadership lay with the educated owners, many of them politicians and bureaucrats, who were versed in classical scholarship and continental ways. These men stood, for at least 150 years, between the era of the master-mason and the era of the architect.

Although gardens feature often enough in medieval stories —notably in the *Roman de la Rose* and in Beauty and the Beast—they do not seem to have been given much attention by builders until the sixteenth century, when they came to be seen as part of the architectural design. At about the same time there came from Italy the idea of a formal garden as a setting for leisured and cultivated conversation. The garden built

Plan of Longford Castle by John Thorpe

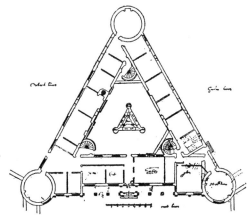

96

A medieval garden

at Theobald's by William Cecil showed both these features. It had impressive architectural ornaments: labyrinths, a fountain, columns, pyramids, and a summer-house with statues of the Roman Emperors. It was 'encompassed with a ditch full of water, large enough for one to have the pleasure of going in a boat and rowing between the shrubs'. Yet it was also a garden in which a man could relax, and Cecil's secretary has left a touching picture of the scene there one day, after the dinner-guests had gone. 'Now we be alone, my lord under a tree in the walks with a book in his hand to keep him from sleeping, and we ready to take bowls into our hands, but that the weather is somewhat too warm yet.'

Such gardens were geometric in their conception, extensions of the houses that they adorned, often enclosed by walls from the outside world. They showed no attempt, such as was fashionable in the nineteenth century, to imitate the informality of nature. Paths were straight, flower-beds either square or shaped in an elaborate 'knot'.

The first English gardening-book—forerunner of countless others—came out in 1563. It was Thomas Hill's *Profitable*

Arte of Gardeninge. Though he had something to say about walks, arbours and mazes, Hill was mainly concerned with practical rather than aesthetic values. The siting of the garden, the time to dig, the time to sow, the best kind of manure, these are the stuff of his book. Full though it is of practical and detailed advice, Hill's list of his own works, given at the end, suggests that he was a literary dilettante rather than a practising expert; they include *The whole art of physiognomy*, *A pleasant Almanack* (which turns out to be on blood-letting), and *The Interpretation of Dreams.* In fact much of his gardening expertise was drawn second-hand from Italian books. Sometimes he even failed to adapt his Italian text to English conditions, telling us blandly that 'the east winds generally be always hotter than the west'!

The habit of gardening spread in the middle and later sixteenth century from the gentry to the yeomen. Harrison said that in his day the 'poor commons' grew melons, cucumbers, radishes, parsnips, carrots, cabbages, turnips, and 'all kinds of salad herbs'. Probably he was thinking of the home counties, which had a hungry market for vegetables in the dining-rooms of London, and where, by the early seventeenth century,

Work and pleasure in a formal garden

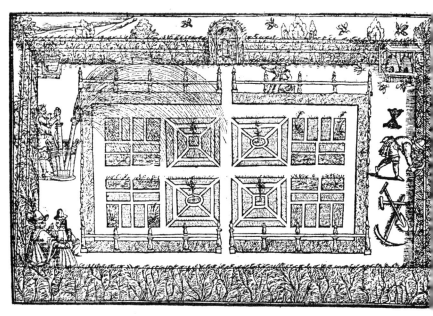

husbandmen were growing 'roses, raspesses, strawberries, gooseberries, herbs for food and physic.' In the further reaches of the country gardens seem to have been unknown to peasants until much later; but we have seen in the later sixteenth century the first beginning of what has long been the Englishman's principal week-end hobby, replaced only in the last few years by the ritual Sunday car-polishing.

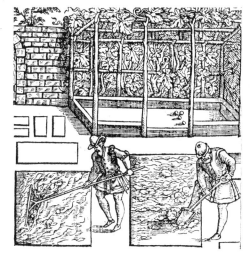

Gardeners raking and digging

Further Reading

E. Mercer, *English Art, 1553-1625*, 1962
James Lees-Milne, *Tudor Renaissance*, 1951
A. Clifton-Taylor, *The Pattern of English Building*, 1962
M. W. Barley, *The English Farmhouse and Cottage*, 1961
John Dent, *The Quest for Nonsuch*, 1962
Frank Jenkins, *Architect and Patron*, 1961

A maze, typical of the geometric patterns

V

Doctors, Disease and Diet

Since the Second World War medical science has advanced so quickly that a whole world of pain seems to be passing away. We can hardly now imagine what life was like, even at the beginning of our own century, when pneumonia and tuberculosis were killers. How much more difficult then to imagine the infinitely more precarious state of life in the sixteenth century! Yet imagine it we must if we are to have any conception of the quality of living and of dying.

From the middle of the fourteenth century, when the Black Death reached England, plague has been the most savage of all killers, an ever-present cloud of anxiety at the back of men's minds. To understand the fears of men and the facts of death between 1348 and 1666 we must analyse this disease, at once repulsive and fascinating, the subject of more than one great book. Of its two main varieties the most infectious was and is pneumonic plague, which attacks the lungs and is spread whenever its victim coughs. The commoner and better-known variety, bubonic plague, seems mild by comparison, yet horrible enough in reality. This type produces monstrous swellings of the lymphatic glands. Its bacilli are seldom spread directly from man to man, but require an intermediary, the flea, *Xenopsylla cheopsis*, whose favourite home is the body of the black rat, but which will sometimes leave its rodent host for man. Pneumonic plague will spread where there are only humans, bubonic plague requires rats and fleas as well. So vague are the medical descriptions of the Middle Ages and the

Tudor period that it is hard to tell which variety was in command at any particular time. However, it seems likely that the Black Death of 1348-9, with its appallingly swift advance, was pneumonic plague, and that at some point bubonic took over. For the epidemics of the fifteenth and sixteenth centuries spread less rapidly than those of the fourteenth and were mostly confined to the towns, where the black rat had his home.

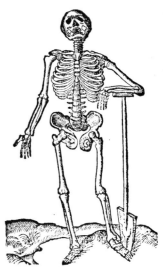

A memento of the plague (from a treatise of 1578)

Contemporaries, of course, knew nothing of all these distinctions. Some saw plague as the agent of God's punishment—and insisted that there was nothing more to be said or done. Others believed that it came from a poisonous miasma in the air. Yet others thought, like a seventeenth-century astrologer, that 'all popular diseases are irritated by Mars and Saturn their influences', and recommended that 'a good nativity is the certainest amulet or antidote that a man can have'. Those who came nearest to modern notions held, with the great Jerome Fracaster, that invisible particles entered the body, bred there, and attacked the tissues. From the mid-seventeenth century to the nineteenth there was to be heated controversy between the apostles of miasma and the apostles of contagion, but in Tudor times there was little debate and many men held two or three contradictory theories at once. Even Fracaster believed that the stars had their influence, and William Shakespeare saw plague as a mixture of planetary conjunction, miasma, and divine vengeance:

> . . . *As a planetary plague, when Jove*
> *Will o'er some high-viced city hang his poison*
> *In the sick air.*

Diagnosis and remedy altered unknowingly, according to the variety of plague that was prevalent. With pneumonic, the infection was too obvious to miss and the contagionist theory was uppermost: isolation and quarantine were sensibly advised.

With bubonic, the miasmic theory was dominant and men were recommended, wisely enough as it happens, to flee the poisoned air of the towns for the countryside. In escaping the air, they also escaped the rats. Henry VIII once cunningly used this theory to bring a committee of theologians to make a decision—never an easy task. Himself safe in Windsor, he told the clerics that they must stay in plague-infected London until they had made up their minds, deaf to Archbishop Cranmer's plea that 'they die at my gate, even at the next house to me'.

In the course of the sixteenth century the central government and the local councils elaborated precautions against the plague. In 1543 London aldermen were ordered to paint the sign of the cross on every afflicted house; any infected person was to stay indoors for 40 days; the inhabitants of infected houses were to burn all straw and bedding; no 'housekeeper' should eject a diseased person from his house without providing other lodging; all dogs, except hounds, spaniels, and mastiffs, were to be destroyed; beggars were to be kept out of churches; and the streets were to be cleaned. Twenty-five years later these instructions were expanded into the beginnings of State welfare. An 'honest, discreet person' was to be appointed for providing quarantined households with necessities at the householder's cost; aldermen were to collect money from the rich in order to give food to the afflicted poor; and a form of medical service appeared with the order that attention to the sick be given by 'the best learned in physic within this realm . . . and without charge to the meaner sort of people.'

Plague sufferers were offered various remedies. One recipe suggested two pounds of figs, two handfuls of rue, and 60 walnuts blanched and beaten small—a tedious task. If this did not work the patient could try roasted onions filled with treacle and pepper. The preachers too had their nostrums: 'take a pound of good hard penance, and wash it well with the water of your eyes. . . .' Some clerics even insisted that any remedy other than prayer was sinful, since plague came directly from God; but such men had a sharp reprimand from the government, which forbade the teaching of this doctrine.

No wonder that in this state of medical science the plague

spread panic! At its approach people fled on 'wagons, carts, and horses, full laden with young bairns, for fear of the Black Pestilence, with their boxes of medicines and sweet perfumes'. One of the characters in William Bullein's *Dialogue against the Fever Pestilence* complained that 'the daily jangling and ringing of the bells, the coming in of the minister to every house in ministering the communion, the reading of the homily of death, the digging up of graves,

Treating a patient

the sparring of windows, and the blazing forth of the blue crosses do make my heart tremble and quake.' The Recorder of London told Lord Burghley how, 'being sent by the lords [of the Privy Council] to search for lewd persons in sundry places, he found dead corpses under the table, which surely did greatly annoy him'. Some men reacted to an epidemic with prayer, others with merry-making:

Some streets had churches full of people, weeping:
Some others Taverns had, rude-revel keeping.

Plague was not the only terror. In 1485 there had suddenly appeared a new disease, the 'sweating sickness'. 'As it found them, so it took them; some in sleep, some in wake, some in mirth, some in care, some fasting, and some full, some busy and some idle.' Four more epidemics followed and then, after the last in 1551, the disease mysteriously disappeared. Short-lived as it was, it has its monument, for John Caius, founder of Gonville and Caius College, Cambridge, wrote on it the first book in English that gives a detailed observation of a specific disease. In his *Book against the Sweating Sickness*, he says that the illness starts with a sweat and a fever. It can be diagnosed by pains in back or shoulder; then follow pains in liver and

Cleaning the House

stomach; 'thirdly by the pain in the head and madness [i.e. delirium] of the same; fourthly by the passion [i.e. palpitations] of the heart.'

Another, and longer-staying, immigrant was smallpox, which came to England in 1514, when Henry VIII was ill with a disease *'nommée la petite verolle'*. Since many writers in Tudor England thought measles and smallpox to be varieties of the same illness, it is not easy to be sure of its course. But one famous victim it certainly had. On 15th October 1562 William Cecil was summoned to Hampton Court where the royal doctors told him that Elizabeth was in danger of death. By the next evening she had fallen into a coma and lay 'without speech'; yet at midnight the fever seemed to be cooling and by the following morning the eruption of spots had come out and all was well.

These diseases prompted some reform of the dirt and stench of our houses, which so shocked foreign visitors, among them Erasmus. 'The floors', he said, 'are made of clay and are covered with layers of rushes, constantly replenished, so that the bottom layer remains for twenty years harbouring spittle, vomit, the urine of dogs and men, the dregs of beer, the remains of fish, and other nameless filth'. Typical of the efforts at improvement was an order made by the corporation of Ludlow that all inhabitants 'shall from time to time sweep and keep clean the street before their doors unto the channel of the said street, and that no muck or dunghill be here suffered to remain above the space of two hours'. Even if the order was obeyed, the smell of Ludlow's streets can have been none too sweet.

Bodies were not much cleaner than houses. Although the Greeks and Romans regarded bathing as a central part of social life, the habit had been abandoned in the Middle Ages until the crusaders brought back from the east the idea of public baths. Eighteen Turkish baths, known as 'stews', were then built in Southwark; but as they rapidly came to be used as brothels too,

104

Henry VIII had them suppressed. 'If', ran the proclamation, 'there be any house wherein is kept and holden any hot-house or sweating-house, for ease and health of men, to which be resorting or conversant any strumpets or women of evil name or fame . . .', then that house must be closed. Henry may have improved London's morals, but he killed its public baths until they revived at the end of the following century. Only in spas like Bath did they continue. There public bathing certainly became very popular among the gentry, and a great deal of money was spent on 'sundry curious pieces of workmanship' to make the baths cleaner and more comfortable. But men went to Bath to cure their agues, not to wash their bodies.

Men may not have been getting any cleaner, but their houses probably were. The smelly garderobes of medieval castles were now being abandoned for 'stool-houses', each with its close-stool—a sort of commode. At Ingatestone Hall Sir William Petre built five stool-houses and a most elaborate system of water-pipes and drains, making 'divers vaults and gutters of brick, very large, under the ground, round about the whole situation of the house, conveying the waters from every office'. He also brought in a supply of 'very clear and sweet' water to

Sir William Petre's drainage system at Ingatestone Hall, Essex, 1565

'every office of the house'. Probably Petre was advanced in his ideas of hygiene, for Ingatestone was built 50 years before Sir John Harington, the Queen's godson, devised his water-closet, which did not really catch on until the eighteenth century. Even so, Petre's plans show the lines on which upper-class builders were thinking.

The doctoring available in Tudor times does not inspire any more confidence today than does the hygiene. Then, as now, the medical profession was highly conscious of the differences in status within itself. Physicians lorded it over surgeons, and both lorded it over apothecaries. The three groups were indeed entirely different in their training, methods, and social rankings. The physicians were university men, thoroughly grounded in the classics and in the standard text-books of Galen and other doctors of the ancient world. Their qualifications were high, for they had to know—besides physiology—grammar, rhetoric, logic, geometry, and above all astronomy. But they were content to inhabit an academic ivory tower, often enough prescribing for a patient without even seeing him, and basing their remote diagnosis upon the prevailing theory of humours. Each man was thought to be compounded of four humours, blood, phlegm, yellow bile, and black bile, with the attendant complexions—sanguine, phlegmatic, choleric, and melancholic. Illness came when the humours got unbalanced, and this could be detected at a distance by examination of the patient's urine: if it was too thin, water in the bowels was 'betokened', and so on. With the process of water-casting established as the foundation of the doctor's art, the typical picture of the sixteenth-century doctor shows him gazing at his urine flask, rather as

The apothecary

the doctor of today is usually imagined with his stethoscope.

Doctor testing urine

Treatment was based upon the same theory. If there were an imbalance of humours, then the surplus must be let out, generally by blood-letting. This could be done by opening a vein, or by 'cupping'—that is to say, by placing a hot cup over the victim's skin—or, for wealthy patients only, by applying leeches to suck the blood. But we should not imagine that bleeding was a simple process, for it had to be done in accordance with the phases of the moon, and here of course that essential item of the physician's education, astronomy, played its part.

The surgeon was quite a different sort of man. Drawn from a lower social rank, with little education, he was above all a craftsman, carrying out the instructions of the learned physician. In the Middle Ages physicians had normally been priests, forbidden by Pope Innocent III to shed blood and consequently forced to use assistants, who were usually in the early days barbers. This gave an opportunity to the surgeons. While physicians needed a university degree in the classics, surgeons needed principally 'a good eye and a steadfast hand'. They learned their trade by practising it, and their approach, brutal as it often was, at least remained unhampered by academic theorising. 'Chirurgery', said Ambroise Paré, the greatest of them all, 'is not learnt in the study, chirurgery is learnt by the eye and by the hands.'

Both physicians and surgeons were much occupied, as they are today, with excluding quacks and interlopers. In 1518 the College of Physicians was founded to keep out of medical practice 'common artificers, as smiths, weavers, and women who boldly and customarily take upon themselves great cures . . . in which they use sorcery and apply medicines very noyous'. Considering the scale of the physicians' fees it is not surprising that people flocked to the quacks, attracted by advertisements like this: 'if any man, woman, or child, be sick or would be let blood, or be diseased with any manner of inward or outward griefs, as all manner of agues or fevers, pleurisies, colic, stone, strangulation . . . let them resort to the Saracen's Head in the East Lane and they shall have remedy by me'. Clearly all the regulations of the physicians were inadequate to suppress these charlatans. The surgeons, although of lesser status, were equally anxious to keep out interlopers, or, as they put it, to protect laymen, who could not distinguish 'the uncunning from the cunning'—the word 'cunning' had not then any pejorative overtone and simply meant 'skilful'. One surgeon angrily listed the quacks who claimed to practise his craft: 'now-a-days it is apparent to see how tinkers, tooth-drawers, pedlars, ostlers, carters, porters, horse-gelders and horse-leeches, idiots, applesquires, broom-men, bawds, witches, conjurors, soothsayers, and sow-gelders, rogues, rat-catchers, runagates, and proctors of spittle-houses . . . daily abuse both physic and surgery.' At least the sixteenth-century advocates of the closed shop used more entertaining language than they do today! But they did not rely upon words alone, for in 1518 the Barbers Company and the Surgeons Company of London were united into a corporation,

The Barber-Surgeons Company receiving its charter

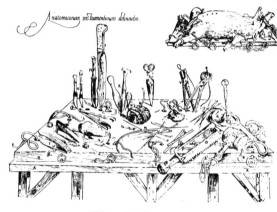

grandiloquently known as 'the Masters or Governors of the Mystery and Comminalty of Barbers and Surgeons of London'. This event was celebrated in Holbein's famous and symbolic picture of Henry VIII handing to the barbers and surgeons their new charter—a ceremony that seems never in fact to have taken place.

Dissecting instruments

The foundation of the College of Physicians and of the Barber-Surgeons Company marked the beginning of a slow advance in medical practice. Although a student had still to enter a foreign university in order to find any adequate instruction in his subject, the education of physicians began now to improve a little. The lectures started in 1546 by Dr Caius were the foundation of advanced medical learning in England, and a few years later the College was granted the privilege of using annually the bodies of four executed criminals for its dissections. In some other directions the progress made was more equivocal. One of the great names of sixteenth-century science is that of Auroleus Philip Theophrastus Bombastus von Hohenheim, who preferred, understandably enough, to be known as Paracelsus. A man of vast confidence in his own powers and a remarkable skill in self-advertisement, he yet broke down the old theories of Galen and helped in the long run to prepare the way for great advances. 'You will not', he said, 'find everything written in the books of Galen and Avicenna, all of surgery has not been written, for new times bring new diseases and new books will outmode the old.' The idea that books become out-of-date, readily accepted today, was then startling and revolutionary. So was Paracelsus' notion that 'you must learn daily from your own experience and from the experience of others'. Such advice was sound enough, but unfortunately the things that he learned and the theories that he made fashionable

109

can only have harmed his patients. One of his firmest beliefs was in the doctrine of signatures, which taught that the curative 'virtues' of plants can be discovered from their appearance. Thus, because the flowers of St John's Wort resembled blood when putrified, they must be good for dressing wounds. Another fashion started by Paracelsus was the notion that each plant was a terrestrial star. Sowing and gathering had therefore to be done at the right astronomical moment. For instance, herbs intended to benefit a male patient should be gathered when the sun or the moon was in a male sign—Sagittarius or Aquarius or Leo. Such were the views held by some of the most advanced medical theorists in sixteenth-century England.

Real advances in medical theory had to wait upon the work of Harvey in the next century, but there was meanwhile some progress made on the technical and practical side. In Italy fascinating work had been done on anatomy by Vesalius, and his descriptions were ruthlessly pirated in England by Thomas Geminus. However much one may regret Geminus' professional ethics, one must admire the skill and artistry with which he presented his work to the English public. In his *Compendiosa Totius Anatomiae delineatio*, filled with exact and beautiful engravings that uncover the body layer by layer, Renaissance art and the craft of printing wonderfully combined to further the science of medicine. Printing was indeed of great value in spreading medical knowledge and the large number of books produced is testimony to public interest in the subject. One of the most remarkable of these was Thomas Phaire's *Boke of Chyldren*, the first printed English book on pediatrics. Phaire believed that it was better to spread knowledge widely than to keep it hidden, and in days when there were few doctors, many quacks and multitudinous diseases, one cannot doubt that he was right. Like so many of its contemporaries, his book is a curious mixture of sense and fantasy.

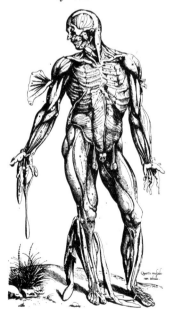

Anatomical drawing of muscles, by Geminus

110

Seeing the importance of a baby's earliest days in forming its character, Phaire recommended that mothers should feed their own children. If that were not possible, the foster-nurse should be 'sober, honest, and chaste, well-formed, amiable, and cheerful, so that she may accustom the infant unto mirth; no drunkard, vicious, nor sluttish, for such corrupteth the nature of the child.' This seems

A birth

thoroughly sensible, but one's confidence is weakened when he recommends that, for increasing a mother's milk, 'the powder of earth-worms dried and drunken in the broth of a neat's tongue is a singular experiment'. Singular indeed!

The most striking progress and the most impressive techniques appeared in the despised art of surgery. This was already quite advanced, for complicated operations had long been known—trepanning, for instance, had been practised in prehistoric times and was traditionally used for curing head injuries, epilepsy, and migraines. On this foundation some remarkable innovators were able to build. Perhaps the greatest medical figure of the century, possibly the only one who certainly and consistently did his patients any good, was the French surgeon, Ambroise Paré. Unable to become a physician because of his lack of Latin, Paré became an

Straightening a crooked arm

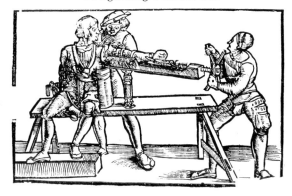

A military dressing station

army surgeon, and this led to his first and greatest discovery. Bullet wounds were then thought to be poisoned by gunpowder and had therefore to be cauterised —with a mixture of boiling oil and treacle. At the battle of Turin in 1538 this mixture luckily ran out, and Paré applied instead a salve made up from yolk of eggs and oil of roses. Not surprisingly the patients so treated recovered more rapidly than those subjected to boiling oil. From this point onwards Paré experimented endlessly. His approach was not always scientific—he was delighted to prise out of a Turin surgeon the recipe for a salve made by boiling 'young whelps new pupped, in oil of lilies [with] earthworms prepared with turpentine of Venice'. But he had an intensely practical and searching mind, which led him to the invention of a truss for hernia, artificial limbs for the disabled, and instruments for healing fractures and dislocations.

Paré was the most famous surgeon of his day, achieving his fame in part because he was a better writer than the more highly educated physicians, who tried to ban his books on the ground that they were not written in Latin. But there were others in Europe working towards a highly developed art. Pierre Franco took his craft beyond the field of wound-surgery into the field of operative surgery, which had until then been the province of quacks, and developed sophisticated techniques for treating hernia, while Gaspare Tagliacozzi created, alone, the science of plastic surgery.

English surgeons were slow to follow this lead. But from the incorporation of the Barber-Surgeons Company in 1540 their training began to improve with the lectures that were given at Barber-Surgeons Hall every Tuesday. One of the lecturers, Thomas Gale, brought out in 1563 his *Certain Works of Chirurgerie*, perhaps the earliest book on the subject to be printed in English. It was not a great book, but it did set out certain simple and modest principles. More remarkable was Gale's successor in the lectureship, William Clowes, who showed an interesting use of experimental method in the long controversy over whether or not gunshot wounds were poisoned. Chapter 13 of the *Profitable and Necessarie Booke of Observations* deals with the case of 'A Lieutenant who was shot in the right buttock with a poisoned bullet' and describes Clowes' empirical investigation of the problem.

These English surgeons of the Tudor age were not, by continental standards, very remarkable. But they were, with others, responsible for bringing over foreign ideas and for developing an interest in medical education that, in the seventeenth century, helped to produce men of European reputation, like William Harvey. They were too the fruit of a growing demand for medical treatment from the general public. Licences to practise were granted in increasing numbers, and many other men were practising without licence. Country towns had by the end of the sixteenth century their little colonies of practitioners, and if the licensed graduates could

Surgical operation, as illustrated by Thomas Gale

not meet the demand, men soon found others who would. Recriminations were savage, as the graduates tried, with little success, to keep out their rivals. The whole business shows how wealthy sections of society were demanding more specialised services and were thus bringing into being something like a nation-wide medical profession.

Obviously the foundation of health was, and is, diet. This was perfectly well realised in the sixteenth century with its elaborate dietary theories, based, like medical theories, upon the doctrine of humours. Old men were phlegmatic, that is to say cold and moist, and should therefore not be given lamb, which was also thought to be phlegmatic. Children too were phlegmatic and should be given hot, moist diets; but as they grew up they became sanguine or choleric, and should therefore have 'grosser' meats and salads. Fruit was looked on with suspicion: 'all fruits', said Sir Thomas Elyot in his *Castle of Health*, 'generally are noyful to man, and do engender ill humours'. Milk was thought 'especially good for them which be oppressed with melancholy, which is a common calamity of students'.

How far such theories were followed in practice it is hard to say—probably not much more than their twentieth-century equivalents are really followed today. The poor could hardly afford to pick and choose, the rich were tempted by greed. For the food of the English nobility was thought by foreigners quite exceptional in its quality. 'The English', said a Venetian ambassador, 'being great epicures and very avaricious by nature, indulge in the most delicate fare themselves, and give their household the coarsest bread and beer.' Englishmen in turn looked on the Scots as even more greedy than themselves, being much occupied in 'large tabling and belly-cheer'. Just as they do today, the English aristocracy employed as cooks what Harrison called 'musical-headed Frenchmen and strangers'. The variety of their menus was incredible: beef, mutton, veal, lamb, kid, pork, rabbit, capon, pig, venison, and fish appeared on the table together. But it is a relief to know that each member of the large assembly of guests and retainers chose from the display the dish that he liked best, what was

A feast

over being then sent out for the servants. The variety of food was matched by a variety of drink, but again the drinking was more moderate than one might have thought, for a man's glass did not stay by his side throughout the meal but was handed to him by a servant from the side-board when he felt thirsty. Talk was similarly restrained, merchants and artificers being despised for talking too much at their feasts and telling doubtful stories. That some people may, however, have found upper-class meals rather boring is suggested by an entry in the *Grete Herball* of 1529: 'to make folk merry at the table take four leaves and four roots of vervain in wine, then sprinkle the wine all about the house . . . and they shall be all merry.' It might be worth trying.

But such accounts are of feasts. What did great households eat on ordinary days? In Sir William Petre's house at Ingate-stone the menu was generally solid enough. In Christmas week, 1551, when the Petres themselves were away, a typical dinner for about 20 servants consisted of three pieces of boiled beef, one piece of roast meat, a coney and a partridge; for supper that day they had five joints of mutton and another coney. After Christmas, when both Petre and his wife had come home, the ordinary menu was more varied: boiled beef, a leg of pork, a chine of beef, a shoulder of venison, and a coney for dinner; nine joints of mutton, a capon, four coneys, two teals, and a woodcock for supper. In Lent the fast was strictly kept: ling, haberdin, mudfish and herring made up a typical menu. Only the children and the sick got any relief from the eternal fish.

On ordinary days merchants ate much more moderately than the nobility—two or three courses seem to have been normal. But at feasts they set out to impress. The butcher's usual joints were rejected, delicate meats were ordered from all parts of the kingdom, and tables were garnished with gingerbreads, tarts, 'florentines', and jellies. 'The kind of meat which is obtained with most difficulty and cost is commonly taken for the most delicate', said Harrison severely. But this was in the reign of Elizabeth, and it is likely that earlier in the century the meals of such people were large without being fabulous.

Artisans in the towns and yeomen in the country feasted rather less often and, when they did, each guest would bring a contribution. Their staple foods were black bread, milk, cheese, and eggs, with occasional dishes of poultry or bacon. The daily diet of a fifteenth-century peasant has been reckoned as one pint of milk, one pint of whey, two ounces of cheese, one ounce of bacon, two pounds of bread, and two ounces of pease. As the following century drew on, however, the food of the well-to-do yeoman became more varied and more appetising than this; he could now afford more meat, and, like the present-day American, began to reject chicken in favour of beef and mutton. But the poorer peasants and workmen were by contrast going hungry. The price of their foods was shooting up in the middle of the Tudor era: 'within these eight years you could buy the best pig or goose that I could lay my hands on for fourpence, which now cost me eightpence.' For those who depended upon wages for their livelihood the inflation of the sixteenth century may well have reduced the standard of living to its lowest point in the last 700 years.

What was the quality of this food? And how healthy was the diet? In a very rough way one can divide the English population of Tudor times into meat-eaters and bread-eaters—although of course the rich ate some bread and the poor ate some meat. There were more kinds of meat available then than there are today, for few of us eat much venison and none of us, I hope, eat sea-gulls, cranes, or bustards. But its quality was probably a good deal worse. Meat for the winter was usually taken from animals slaughtered in the autumn and it had therefore to be salted or pickled. In the summer it was eaten 'fresh', but without refrigeration it may

Buying eggs in the market

often have been tainted. To make salted meat palatable and to disguise the taint of 'fresh' meat, cooks had to use all the seasoning, sauces, and spices that they could; and it is no surprise that fortunes could be made out of the trade in pepper.

Sixteenth-century bread was very different from our own. The finest wheaten bread, reserved for the well-to-do, was made from wholemeal flour, containing some bran and the germ of the wheat. Unlike our own white bread, from which the nutritious germ has been laboriously extracted, this was creamy-yellow in colour. Less expensive wheaten breads were darker, since more of the bran was left in the flour by the miller. Dark brown or black bread, the food of servants and peasants, was made either from maslin, a mixture of rye and wheat, or from drage, a mixture of barley and wheat, or from rye alone, or, in the north, from oats. In time of famine the poor were reduced to 'horse-corn' a bread made from beans, peas, lentils and oats. As time went on the fashion for wheaten bread spread down the social scale. In 1621 Sir Symonds d'Ewes remarked rather sourly that 'the poorer sort traversed

117

A dining-room

the markets to find out the finest wheats, for none else would now serve their use'. Since the end of the eighteenth century all English bread has been made from wheat alone and black rye bread is now a recherché food imported for Englishmen with cosmopolitan tastes. The high-protein diet of the meat-eating rich was probably not very healthy. They seem to have eaten little fruit and may well have suffered from mild forms of scurvy—frequent complaints about loose teeth and rotting gums suggest as much. Probably more serious was a deficiency of vitamin A, which is derived from green vegetables, milk, butter, and eggs. Green vegetables were seldom eaten by anyone in the sixteenth century, and the rich seem to have despised milk, butter and eggs as the food of peasants. This may well have been the cause of stones in the bladder and the urinary tract, from which many of the gentry suffered. Excess may, however, have been more damaging than deficiencies, and if the well-to-do in Tudor England really ate the amount of rich food claimed for them, it is not surprising that they complained so constantly of ill health. The health record of Sir William Petre is typical. When he was about 40 he had a 'flux' in his leg—probably a varicose ulcer—which troubled him for the rest of his life. A little later he developed a stone in the kidney and a rupture. After Elizabeth's accession, when he was 52, the stone became very much worse and nearly killed him. By the age of 60 he was saying that 'I account myself unfit to be in any company', for he was too deaf to hear what was being said and unable to move about except with great discomfort.

The traditional peasant diet was probably adequate and healthy. 'Old' Parr of Shropshire was said by his poetical biographer to have thought

That green cheese was most wholesome (with an onion)
Coarse maslin bread; and for his daily swig,
Milk, butter-milk and water, whey and whig,
Sometimes metheglin, and by fortune happy,
He sometimes sipp'd a cup of ale most nappy.

Since Parr was convicted of fornication at the age of 105 and did not die until his presentation at court at the age of 152, his diet clearly had its virtues. But how often was this standard attained? Harrison mentioned the poor who were sometimes forced to make bread of 'horse-corn' or even of acorns; and it is very likely that towns and countryside suffered from periodic famines. But the inarticulate and the starving do not leave us their diet-sheets.

Further Reading

W. S. C. Copeman, *Doctors and Disease in Tudor Times*, 1960
Lawrence Wright, *Clean and Decent*, 1960
L. F. Hirst, *The Conquest of Plague*, 1953
J. C. Drummond and Anne Wilbraham, *The Englishman's Food*, 1957
W. J. Ashley, *The Bread of our Forefathers*, 1928

VI

School and College

Since education is concerned with fitting men and women for particular roles in society and moulding them according to the ideal types of the time, its history can only be understood in relation to social demands and aspirations. In the Middle Ages the dominant figure among laymen had been the knight, portrayed sometimes as man-at-arms, sometimes as the lover of romance, sometimes as the seeker after the holy grail. In the course of the sixteenth century this ideal type was replaced by another, the English gentleman, whose appearance mirrors new values and hopes in society. Yet the change was far from rapid. The Englishman's favourite reading at the end of the fifteenth century was Malory's *Morte d'Arthur*, chosen by Caxton for the regeneration of the governing classes and the revival of English greatness. Malory had been brought up in the train of Richard Beauchamp, earl of Warwick, the last great English champion of medieval chivalry. In his superb prose epic Malory largely ignored the religious and romantic elements of the Arthurian story, using the legend to establish models of the noble soldiers who might rescue England from the degradation of defeat in France. To such appeals his countrymen were still ready to respond: Henry VII named his eldest son Arthur, while Henry VIII devised a great pageant of knighthood in the Field of the Cloth of Gold.

During the sixteenth century this ideal of chivalry came to be fiercely derided. Roger Ascham, for instance, called it 'open manslaughter and bold bawdry'. The humanist and diplomat,

Richard Pace, spoke with contempt of the landowner who told him that 'gentlemen's sons ought to be able to blow their horn skilfully, to hunt well, and to carry and train a hawk elegantly, but the study of letters is to be left to the sons of peasants'. By the reign of Elizabeth such an attitude had become archaic. However poorly educated the sons of noblemen might in reality be, everyone recognised that learning was essential. One writer sharply warned the gentry of the dangers of ignorance: 'alas, you will be un-

Hunting, the accomplishment of the old-style gentleman

gentle gentlemen, if you be no scholars; you will do your prince but simple service, you will stand your country but in slender stead, you will bring yourselves but to small preferment, if you be no scholars.'

The ideal gentleman should still be a man of honour and he should be able to fight. But he must also be able to bear the burdens of civil government, and for that purpose he had to be lettered. The power, prestige, and profit that went with government, the gentleman's obligation to rule, and the new fashions of renaissance humanism impelled the upper classes to seek education.

But this was not the only impulse behind the spread of letters. To the devout Protestant ignorance was the seed-bed of Popery: only learning could withstand the snares of Rome and lead men to true religion. Education itself ministered to the glory of God, since, to quote from a funeral sermon for a schoolmaster, 'all secular learning is the knowledge of God's works, . . . a small emanation from eternal verity'. It helped the children of the poor to lead a virtuous life, and without it many children 'fell to idleness and lived dissolutely all their days'.

This serious tone marked discussion of every stage of a child's upbringing. Training for life should begin at the earliest moment, and Sir Thomas Elyot insisted that 'noblemen's children, . . . from the wombs of their mother, shall be made propise [i.e. fit] or apt to the governance of a public weal'. He pointed out that children readily imitated others, and, 'whiles they be tender and the little slips of reason begin in them to burgeon, there may hap by evil custom some pestiferous dew of vice to pierce the said members'. They must therefore be isolated from all bad company: the foster-nurse must be carefully chosen, no men except the doctor may be allowed in the nursery, play-fellows must not do 'any reproachable act or speak any unclean word'. People in the sixteenth century did not so much believe that the child was father to the man as that the child was the man in miniature. The clothes of both boys and girls were tiny versions of the dress of their elders and a high standard of discipline was demanded. Within the family the father's law was strict and long maintained. Control, even in a household like Sir Thomas More's, was firmly if lovingly applied. But although the tone of the conduct books was stern, children had their toys, games and songs, and were often led gently from play to learning. They must be 'sweetly allured', in Elyot's words, 'with praises and such pretty gifts as children delight in'.

There has been a great deal of argument about

Children in adult dress: Lady Sidney and her family

the fate of English schools in the Tudor period. Some historians have asserted that a great revival began in the early sixteenth century and was fostered by the Reformation, others that the dissolution of the chantries under Edward VI destroyed rather than created schools. The truth

Children at play

remains obscure; but it seems likely that argument about the role of the Reformation has led historians to ignore the steady progress made by education from the mid-fifteenth to the mid-seventeenth century.

Medieval England had known many schools, the earliest based on monasteries, others controlled by cathedrals and collegiate churches, later ones attached to chantries. Had all the institutions which once existed before 1450 been still flourishing at that date all would have been well. But it seems that by then many schools had died or declined. In London, where no school could be established without the consent of the bishop of London and the chancellor of St Paul's, clerical monopoly had so effectively kept out interlopers that by 1440 the city had only three grammar schools, all of them in decline. Nor does the picture seem to have been much more cheerful in the rest of the country. But low as the state of education was in the first part of the fifteenth century, the movement had already begun which was to break the clerical monopoly and to give England by 1600 a magnificent range of grammar schools. In the late fourteenth century William of Wykeham had founded Winchester, where the masters were priests, but the school independent of any clerical body. The corporation of 'warden, scholars, and clerks' was a self-governing community, part of a great educational scheme whose other half was New College, Oxford. Modelled upon and rivalling Winchester was Henry VI's foundation at

Eton, intended to 'excel all other grammar schools' and to 'be called the lady, mother and mistress of all other grammar schools'. Interesting, but most unusual, was the school founded at Sevenoaks in 1432, where the statutes laid down that the Headmaster should be a Bachelor of Arts, 'but by no means in holy orders'. Such schools were the precursors. Masters were still mostly priests, schools were often founded, as Eton was, in conjunction with chantries where masses could be said for the family of the founder. But gradually control was passing away from the institutions of the Church. Dean Colet's re-foundation of St Paul's school pointed the way most clearly. The government of the new school was entrusted, in Erasmus' words, 'to the Company of Mercers, men of probity and reputation', because Colet 'found less corruption in such a body of citizens than in any other order or degree of mankind'. St Paul's was the most famous foundation of Henry VIII's reign, but it was certainly not the only one. In 1541, for instance, John Incent, another dean of St Paul's, founded a school at Berkhamsted in Hertfordshire, later described as 'so strong and fair that the like Grammar School for that point is not to be seen in the whole realm of England'.

Admittedly the fame of St Paul's and the number of schools

The Grammar School, Taunton, built by Bishop Foxe of Winchester

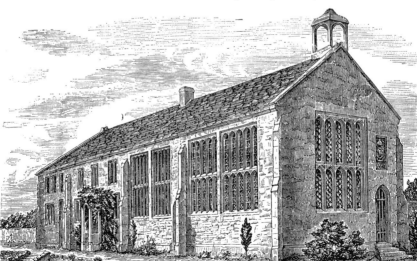

bearing the name of Edward VI have between them given Henry VIII and his son too prominent a place in the history of English education. Certainly the dissolution of the monasteries by Henry and the destruction of the chantries by Edward killed some schools. But by and large their reigns were important in the long process of founding and endowing schools which stretched from the mid-fifteenth century, through the Tudor period, to reach a climax under the early Stuarts. In the 200 years from 1480 to 1660 fifteen grammar schools, with places for 1,500 boys, were founded in London alone.

John Colet (1467–1519), founder of St Paul's School

With the growth of schools the separate profession of school-master was appearing. It was not yet a large profession, since few schools had more than two teachers, a master and an usher, while some had only one. But no longer was the schoolmaster simply a priest who did some teaching. He might or might not be in orders, for some schools preferred a priest, others a layman, but he was generally a man who would devote his full attention to the school. His salary was not high, but under Elizabeth the master's stipend averaged about £15 per annum, which was rather better than the standard for a parish priest, while the usher averaged about £9.

Schoolmasters were still looked upon with some suspicion and outspoken rules were framed for their conduct. The statutes of Shrewsbury School laid down that the masters were not to be 'common gamesters, nor common haunters of taverns or alehouses, or other suspect houses'. At Witton, near Northwich, the founder, Sir John Dean, ordained that the master should have a university degree and be at least 30 years old. He went on to say that 'it is the greatest hindrance to the scholars to have a schoolmaster that is negligent in his office, or doth not profit his scholars, dissolute in manners, a drunkard, a

Seal of Wimborne Grammar School

whoremonger, or entangled with other occupations repugnant to his vocation, a dicer or a common gamester.' Incontrovertible principles! But it seems a little odd that they should have needed establishing. The positive qualities required were depicted in the statutes of St Saviour's, Southwark: 'he shall be a man of a wise, sociable, and loving disposition, not hasty or furious, nor of any ill example; he shall be wise and of good experience to discern the nature of every several child, to work upon their disposition for the greatest advantage, benefit, and comfort of the child, to learn with the love of his book, if such a one may be got.' If, indeed! These statutes were not, of course, the only guides to the proper conduct of a teacher. For a professional literature was now beginning to appear, headed by Roger Ascham's deservedly famous *Schoolmaster*.

It is difficult to discover much about elementary education. In the early part of the sixteenth century parish and chantry priests seem to have been mainly responsible for teaching children to read and write. But from the middle of the century the parish clergy seem no longer to have accepted this duty. Some grammar schools took over the task themselves. For instance, at Burford School there were to be 'grammarian scholars' and 'petties', so that every man in the parish 'minding to set his child to school . . . should be taught his ABC, his catechism, primer, and to read and write'. But other schools refused to accept any pupil who had not already passed beyond this stage. The statutes of St Paul's enjoined the master to 'first see that they can [say] the Catechism in English or Latin, and that every of the said two hundred and fifty scholars can read perfectly and write competently; or else let them not be admitted in no wise.' But of the schools at which they became qualified little evidence has survived.

Fortunately we know much more about the grammar schools. Most boys came when they were about seven and left by the time they were fifteen. although some of course left much earlier. While there they were subjected to an unremitting regime of work. There were only two short vacations: about two-and-a-half weeks at Christmas and two weeks at Easter. During the rest of the year, school went on for six days in the week. In summer the day ran from 6.0 a.m. until 11.0 a.m. and then from 1.0 p.m. until 5.0 p.m. or 6.0 p.m.; in winter it generally started an hour later and occasionally finished an hour earlier. At some schools holidays or half-holidays, aptly called 'remedies', were granted as often as once a week, but even so it has been lugubriously calculated that a schoolboy spent 1,826 hours in school each year.

Discipline was usually harsh. Probably fairly typical was the experience of Thomas Tusser, the agricultural poet, who wrote of his schooldays:

> *O painful time, for every crime,*
> *What 'toesed' ears, like baited bears,*
> *What bobbed lips, what jerks, what nips.*

Not for nothing was the birch often shown on the school seal. But there were some reforming schoolmasters, like Queen Elizabeth's tutor, Roger Ascham, who believed that 'young children were sooner allured by love, than driven by beating, to attain good learning'. There were some fortunate pupils, like Lady Jane Grey, whose tutor, Mr Elmer, 'teacheth me so gently, so pleasantly, with such fair allurements to learning, that I think all the time nothing whilst I

Corporal punishment

am with him'. Consequently she preferred Plato to hunting and conveniently proved Ascham's point.

Latin, with Greek in some schools, was the main subject in the curriculum. Indeed apart from study of the Scriptures it was often the only school subject. In the Middle Ages knowledge of Latin had been a practical necessity for the professional man. Only in Latin could priest or diplomat conduct his business; only with Latin could theologian, lawyer or doctor read his essential texts. From the sixteenth century onwards, with the growing use of vernacular languages, Latin came to be less essential as a tool for all trades. Yet it survived as the central school subject. In part of course it continued to have many practical uses; but it came also to claim other, less tangible, values. The humanist scholars urged a deliberate imitation of classical authors, because, according to Ascham, in Greek and Latin 'we find always wisdom and eloquence, good matter and good utterance, never or seldom asunder'. Copy the style of the greatest writers and you will come to imbibe their wisdom.

Master and pupils

But this was the view of an advanced reformer and we can therefore be sure that it was not always heeded. Much of the teaching in schools was simply a hard grounding in Latin grammar, with the classical authors used as quarries for parts of speech rather than models to be imitated. In the Middle Ages this instruction was largely oral; but in the last years of the fifteenth century there appeared printed grammar-books. The most famous of these was written by William Lily, the first headmaster of St Paul's, who in 1540 achieved the ambition of all writers of text-books when his grammar was given a

128

monopoly by royal proclamation. 'We will and command . . . all you school-masters and teachers of grammar,' said Henry VIII, 'as ye intend to avoid our displeasure, and have our favour, to teach and learn your scholars this English introduction, here ensuing, and the Latin grammar annexed to the same, and none other.' Such governmental interference in an academic matter was in no way thought remarkable.

Erasmus of Rotterdam

The syllabus of Latin study somewhat varied from school to school; but the work of the four forms of East Retford may have been fairly typical. The first form, for beginners or 'petits', was taught the ABC, the inflection of Latin nouns and verbs, and a small Latin vocabulary. In the second form boys went on to 'a more full explication of the eight parts of reason, with the syntax or construction', the *Colloquies* of Erasmus, the *Letters* of Cicero, translation of English into Latin, study of the Old and New Testaments, Sallust, Salern, and Justinian's *Institutes*. The third form studied Lily's Grammar, Virgil, Ovid, and Cicero, and the *De Copia* of Erasmus, while making daily translations of English into Latin. The fourth form learned the principles of versifying, wrote Latin epistles, and began Greek and Hebrew grammar, 'if the master were expert in the same'.

Some opportunities were allowed for recreation, which was no doubt badly needed after this gritty routine. At Shrewsbury the boys were allowed to play 'shooting in the long bow and chess play', but no other games except 'running, wrestling, or leaping'. They were, however, encouraged to act, and the Whitsun play of the Shrewsbury boys, produced by their first great headmaster Thomas Ashton, became a feature of the town. In some other schools rebellious instincts were given a safety valve around Christmas and some sort of outbreak became traditional. The statutes of Witton school provided that the pupils 'bar and keep forth of the school the schoolmaster, in such sort as other scholars do in great schools'.

The English universities of the high Middle Ages were essentially guilds of masters of arts engaged upon teaching. Their pupils mostly intended to enter the service of the Church, and perhaps also of the State. To that end they were prepared to undergo four years' training in the liberal arts for their bachelor's degree and a further three for their master's. The first degree was essentially a preparation for higher studies, not as today an end in itself. In the thirteenth century two colleges, Balliol and Merton, had been founded for the teaching, or regent, masters of the university. They were, like All Souls College today, communities for senior members only. The undergraduates lived where they could, in lodgings or inns, and not surprisingly they gained a reputation for fighting and disorder. Some attempt to curb them was made by the foundation of halls and hostels, where the young men could be supervised by a regent master. These halls were not endowed with lands and bore little resemblance to the academic communities found in the later colleges: they were for living not for teaching. Thus the medieval undergraduate lived in rather the same way as the twentieth-century student at a provincial university; but his teacher, if he were a member of Balliol or Merton, did rather better than his modern counterpart at Redbrick.

New College, Oxford: the front quad

Towards the end of the fourteenth century there came a move of great significance for the future of Oxford and Cambridge. William of Wykeham founded a college, New College, which was designed to continue the education of his Winchester schoolboys. His conception was revolutionary, for he founded a single community of boys working for their first degree, young men working for their

Members of New College: the warden with pupils, priests, lay-clerks, choristers and probationers

master's degree, qualified teachers, and doctors. Wykeham understood very well that the pattern of its buildings will form and perpetuate the structure of a community. In the chambers built about the New College quadrangle he provided lodgings for the fellows. Four men lived in each of the ground-floor rooms, three in the first-floor rooms. Their beds were placed in the centre of the room, which was lighted by a single large window, while at each corner was a separate cubicle, lit by a smaller window. This arrangement can still be seen in the outward aspect of the college buildings today, although later generations have added another storey. Thus Wykeham provided the basis for an academic community in which senior members watched over the welfare and education of junior. Their close-knit life can be seen in the drawing, somewhat like a modern college group, executed by Warden Chandler in the fifteenth century.

Wykeham's foundation has been described in detail because its pattern served as the model and the inspiration for much that followed in Oxford and in Cambridge. Dr John Caius, founder of Gonville and Caius College, looking back in 1573 to the earlier part of the century, said that the hostels he could

Christ Church, Oxford in 1566 (founded by Wolsey as 'Cardinal College' in 1525)

remember, once crowded with students, were now 'all deserted and given back into the hands of the townspeople'. The creation of new colleges and the extension of old transformed both universities and killed the halls and hostels. By 1600 the colleges had come to be the greater part of the university, and undergraduates were coralled within these closely supervised communities. This may be one of the reasons why English university students are so docile by comparison with those of the European mainland and Asia.

The colleges, anxious for fees and for the friendship of the great, began to admit a class of man rather different from the medieval clerks. Bishop Waynflete's fifteenth-century foundation at Magdalen, Oxford, allowed that 20 sons of 'noble and powerful personages, being friends of the said college . . . be taken in and admitted . . . to lodgings and commons, without charge or loss to the College itself, but at their own expense or that of their friends.' The way was now open to the gentleman-commoner, to the fee-paying undergraduate. Not many noblemen seem to have taken this opportunity during the fifteenth century, unless they were planning to enter the Church. But from the beginning of the Tudor era entry to the universities was more and more sought after by the sons of noblemen, gentlemen, professional men, and merchants. They came for the wisdom with which to serve the State and reap the rewards of office, for 'such learning as may serve for delight and ornament and such as the want whereof would speak a defect of breeding'.

Not everyone welcomed their arrival. Some noblemen themselves thought that their sons would be better brought up in separate establishments, where they would 'study matters of action meet for present practice, both of peace and war'. Others were shocked by the levity and luxury introduced into the universities by well-born young men. 'Standing upon their reputation and liberty,' said William Harrison, 'they ruffle and roist it out, exceeding in apparel, and banting riotous company.' When they were accused of unseemly behaviour, they 'think it sufficient to say that they be gentlemen, which grieveth many not a little'. Worse still, they excluded the sons of the poor and potential preachers from university places. 'There be none now but great men's sons in colleges,' complained Hugh Latimer, 'and their fathers look not to have them preachers.' This state of affairs had, in Harrison's view, been brought about by bribery. In elections to fellowships 'he that hath most friends, though he be the worst scholar, is always surest to speed'. Even in the grammar schools, when there was a closed scholarship to be had, 'such bribage is made, that poor men's children are commonly shut out'. The sons of the rich got the scholarships and then spent their time on 'little other than histories, tables, dice, and trifles'.

Those who saw the universities as centres of idle licence were not their only critics. Bacon, at the end of the century, thought them dominated by scholasticism, which led only to 'cobwebs of learning', and humanism, concerned 'with the sweet falling of the clauses' rather than 'weight of matter'. Certainly the basis of university study remained medieval well into the seventeenth century. The undergraduate syllabus was wide yet coherent. Each man had to study three arts—logic, rhetoric, ethics—and three sciences—metaphysics, physics, and mathematics. The vocational subjects, theology, medicine, and law, were generally read after a man had taken his first degree. The groundwork of the whole was Aristotelian logic. Dull perhaps it was; but it allowed methodical study of the mechanics of thought and a solid understanding of the principal fallacies. 'Logic', said a tutor, 'teaches the clenched fist, i.e. to argue strictly and straight.' By contrast rhetoric, the art of communication and persuasion, 'teaches the opened hand, i.e. to speak ornately and at length'. It 'teaches the nature of men's passions and affections, how to raise and move them, how to allay, quiet and change them.' It involved the imitation of literary models, the reading of poetry, and the study of history. The methods of teaching were still largely medieval too. Knowledge was passed on by means of lectures. Essential before the days of printing, when only one man in the class possessed the text to be studied, they now had less point. Consequently some of the lecturers neglected their tasks: they 'grow themselves to be idle and given to play and pleasure, become factious and busy in bye-matters'—the university politician was known even then. Audiences became restive and there were complaints of 'the uncomely hemming and hawking at public lectures'. Still, the lecture survived and it remains to this day the main medium of instruction in some universities.

The second principal survival from the Middle Ages into the sixteenth century, the disputation, has now quite disappeared. Yet it sounds altogether a more lively and exciting affair than the lecture. Each undergraduate had to take part in four disputations during his time. They lasted from 1.0 p.m. until 5.0 p.m. with a refreshment break from 3.0 until 4.0. One student was to defend and another to attack some stated propositions. Proceedings were opened by the moderator, an academic umpire, who gave out the propositions. The 'father' or patron of the defender then started a preliminary discussion before handing over to his pupil, who answered one by one the objections of his opponent. The debate may have been formal enough, but the arguments were lively and taut. Nor were the subjects of debate trivial: one recorded disputation was on the proposition that the threat of punishment is a sufficient deterrent of crime. The method of argument was certainly quite different from our own. There were no statistics of crime and punishment; instead there were closely argued syllogisms:

'Whatever is conducive to virtue is *per se* praiseworthy.
But punishment conduces to virtue.
Therefore it is *per se* praiseworthy.'

This sort of thing may not have helped much to solve social problems, but such disciplined and rigorous argument was probably invaluable in sharpening the mind.

The third method of teaching was the declamation. This was the test of rhetoric, as the disputation was the test of logic. Some declamations were produced simply for the tutor, as the weekly essay is produced today, others were public. Written in Latin on such subjects as 'Was C. J. Caesar justly put to death?' they were

The Oxford Schools, scene of the disputations

valuable exercises in language, history, and the arts of persuasion. Style was the heart of the declamation. 'Let your style be clear and perspicuous, smooth and plain', wrote one tutor, 'nervous, and vivid and masculine, not inert, flat, and languid.'

Medieval as the curriculum and the teaching methods mostly were, some changes appeared in the ancient universities during the sixteenth century. Within the colleges there was emerging the beginnings of a tutorial system. William of Wykeham had provided *informatores*, moral tutors perhaps, for New College, and Bishop Waynflete had established college lecturers and tutors for the fee-paying undergraduates at Magdalen. By the second half of the century the college tutor probably had more influence than anyone else upon an undergraduate's education. Every college, according to Harrison, had its tutors and lecturers who 'daily trade up the youth there abiding privately in their halls', so that after 12 terms they may go 'into the common schools and public disputations . . . to try their skills'. Some tutors at least took their duties with proper seriousness: one Cambridge man even 'read a Greek lecture in his bed to certain young students that preferred their nightly studies before their rest and ease'. But tutors did not always get the respect that they considered their due. Undergraduates had to be urged: 'go to your tutor as to your oracle upon all occasions; . . . when you read or speak in your tutor's chamber or elsewhere, take heed of picking your nose, or putting your hat or hand to your face or any such odd, uncouth, or unseemly gesture.'

With the tutor's help the old arts course consisting of grammar, logic, and rhetoric might in some cases be broadened. A few young men were advised to read history, geography, mathematics and astronomy; and at least one tutor provided a list of 40 books for his pupils, covering what we should today regard as general reading. There was even some teaching of modern languages; but the contemporary attitude to such studies shows the intimidating seriousness of the age, for the author of a French grammar recommended his subject as recreation after the main studies: 'when your mind is amazed and dazzled with long reading, you may refresh and disport you in learning this tongue.'

Education in Tudor England was not only a matter of schools and universities, and there were indeed many who believed that the sons of noblemen should not be sent to such institutions at all, but should instead be brought up in aristocractic households. This was traditional English practice. It led the Venetian ambassador to comment that 'the want of affection in the English is strongly manifested towards their children', for, he went on, 'everyone, however rich he may be, sends away his children into the houses of others, whilst he, in return, receives those of strangers into his own'. Sir Thomas More was brought up in the household of Cardinal Morton, who would say to his guests, 'this child here waiting at the table, whosoever shall live to see it, will prove a marvellous man'. Much later, Walter, Earl of Essex, asked Lord Burghley to receive his son Robert: 'I have', he said, 'wished his education to be in your household . . . and that the whole time which he should spend in England in his minority, might be divided in attendance upon my Lord Chamberlain and you.' Robert was to copy the Chamberlain 'in all the actions of his life, tending either to the wars, or to the institution of a nobleman', and to follow Burghley in 'wisdom and gravity'. Thus the use of great households for training the sons of noblemen continued throughout the century.

But there are signs that it was gradually being superseded, or at least supplemented, by grammar schools and universities.

Higher education could be found not only at the universities but also at the Inns of Court. Harrison claimed that to Oxford and Cambridge 'we may in like sort add the third, which is at London . . . where there are sundry famous houses, of which three are called by the name of Inns of the Court, the rest of the Chancery'. They claimed to serve two purposes: to turn out skilled professional lawyers and to round off the liberal education of the ruling classes. Theoretically the traditional structure of discussions, moots, and readings should have provided an excellent education for men intended to serve as justices of the peace. But in the event students were more inclined to the pleasures of the town than their studies, while lecturers preferred showing off before their colleagues to educating the young. Readings, according to Sir Edward Coke, were 'full of new conceits, liker rather to riddles than lectures, which when they are opened they vanish away like smoke'. No wonder that the students stayed away!

To many, perhaps most Englishmen, vocational training was more important than academic. Unhappily little material about this instruction has survived, and there is in any case little space left to discuss it. In law, before a man could practise any trade or craft, he had to serve an apprenticeship. For at least seven years, sometimes more, he had to live in his master's house learning the work, so that in course of time he might hope to become 'free of his craft'. The relationship between master and apprentice was so much a matter of personality that

137

An early technological treatise: William Cuningham's 'Cosmographical Glasse'

generalisation is virtually impossible. Some masters failed to teach their apprentices the trade: one young man served for seven years before discovering that his master's occupation was upholstery and not, as he had thought, drapery. Others neglected their apprentices' comfort: one man was accused of providing a bed 'foul sheeted and full of vermin'. Yet others again treated the apprentice as part of their own families: John Johnson, for instance, was apprenticed to a master, Antony Cave, who as founder of a grammar school and university scholarships, took a full interest in education. Later Johnson married Cave's niece and was taken into partnership.

Apprenticeship was an old form of training by the sixteenth century. We have already noticed, in earlier chapters, some new forms of vocational teaching. The lectures given at the College of Physicians were helping to improve medical skill. Gresham College gave courses in arithmetic, geography, navigation and so on, in an attempt to combine general principles with practical application. Above all, printing allowed a wide diffusion of useful and popular knowledge. Boorde on houses and medicine, Clowes on surgery, Tusser on farming, and Hill on gardening all testified to the urge for knowledge and self-improvement. The list might, if I had the space and the reader had the patience, be infinitely prolonged.

Further Reading

Roger Ascham, *The Scholemaster*, 1570; repr. 1904

A. F. Leach, *The Schools of Medieval England*, 1916. See Joan Simon, 'A. F. Leach on the Reformation' in *British Journal of Educational Studies* nos 3-4, 1954-56

Foster Watson, *The English Grammar Schools to 1660*, 1908

M. H. Curtis, *Oxford and Cambridge in Transition*, 1959

F. Caspari, *Humanism and the Social Order in Tudor England*, 1954

W. T. Costello, *The scholastic curriculum at early seventeenth-century Cambridge*, 1958

R. R. Bolgar, *The Classical Heritage and its Beneficiaries*, 1954

VII

Church and People

At the beginning of the Tudor period there was no reason for
men to think that the Church in England was on the point of
collapse. The Venetian ambassador wrote in about 1500 that
the English 'all attend Mass every day and say many pater-
nosters in public. . . . They always hear Mass on Sunday in
their parish church and give liberal alms.' He found these parish
churches richly furnished: 'above all are their riches displayed
in the church treasures; for there is not a parish church in the
kingdom so mean as not to possess crucifixes, candlesticks,
censers, patens, and cups of silver.' The churches had moreover
been greatly enlarged during the two generations before the
breach with Rome, and in eastern England especially there was
a burst of rebuilding. Some churches, like that at March in
the Isle of Ely, were given rich, gay timber roofs, while at
Peterborough fan-vaulted chapels were built on to the east end
of the cathedral. Some of the most impressive churchbuilding
was the work of kings: Edward IV had begun and Henry VIII
finished St George's Chapel, Windsor, while Henry VII
bequeathed the money for his chapel at Westminster. Had the
Reformation not come when it did, historians might well have
seen in all these works the affirmation of a strong Catholic faith.

But churches were not always built for direct, simple religious
motives, and to judge the matter properly we need to look
inside them. Pre-reformation churches were decorated in a
somewhat bizarre manner: 'in some churches are suspended
the eggs of ostriches and other things which cause admiration

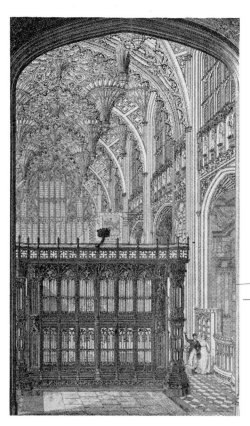
Henry VII's Chapel, Westminster, 1503–19

because rarely seen', wrote a foreigner. Worse than this curio-shop appearance was the habit of using churches as places of assembly. Booths were set up in the nave of Exeter Cathedral during fairs, and St Paul's, London, was always crowded with lawyers, merchants, prostitutes, and pickpockets furthering their trades.

Nor were the rebuilding and decoration of churches necessarily signs of a lively faith. Henry Parker, the fifteenth-century Carmelite friar who wrote *Dives et Pauper*, pointed out that were these things done 'for devotion and for the worship of God . . . I trow this land passed all other lands in worshipping of God and Holy Church. But I dread me that men do it more for pomp and pride of this world to have a name and worship thereby in the country.' A well-appointed church might also be the result of good business. The parishioners of Gresford were understandably proud of their miraculous image of the Virgin, which brought queues of pilgrims and offerings from all over the country, 'by reason whereof . . . the church of the said parish was strongly and beautifully made erect and builded'. Not only that, but 'the inhabitants of the town and parish, with divers others, were not a little aided and favoured towards the better sustentation of their living' by this devoted tourist industry.

The pilgrimages themselves had come to have a superstitious, almost a commercial, element. A man might bequeath money for a pilgrimage to be undertaken in his name by proxy. The

saints to whom the pilgrims flocked were credited with extraordinary powers of helping and of punishing, for holy men
who could cure a disease were also thought capable of inflicting
it: 'who,' said the reformer William Tyndale, 'who dare deny
St Anthony a fleece of wool, for fear of his terrible fire, or lest
he send the pox among our sheep?' Some very strange stories
were put about of miraculous powers. For instance, a bishop
who had been given a block of ice for his gout heard a voice
telling him that within it was a departed soul undergoing
punishment. After he had obligingly celebrated 30 masses the
soul escaped to heaven from its icy prison. At times credulity
was exploited for political purposes. When Wolsey celebrated
mass at the Field of the Cloth of Gold, after the elevation of the
Host 'the Eucharist was seen in the air floating over the
tiltyard, no one perceiving whence it issued nor who propelled
it, to the height of a tall tower . . . to the surprise of those who
did not know how it was done'. Such pantomimes were dis-
approved by serious Catholics as well as by reformers, and
it would be wholly unfair to blacken the Church with everything
that was done in its name. Nor does exposure of commercial
and magical elements imply that all devotion sprang from greed,

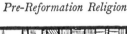

Pre-Reformation Religion

fear and superstition. In most men such motives were, and probably are, mixed with genuine faith. But there are signs that, in the generations before the time of Luther, inner religion was being obscured by a reliance upon the mechanical effects of ritual and invocation.

From these very general comments on the pre-Reformation Church we can turn to the condition and the fate of its various members. What sort of men were the secular clergy of Tudor England? Like any other professional group, then and now, they ranged widely in wealth, ability and integrity. They included flamboyant princes of the Church and threadbare priests, noble martyrs and calculating turncoats. The typical bishop of early Tudor days was an organisation-man rather than a saint. Wolsey, of course, stood by himself in worldly power and riches; but most of his colleagues on the bench also saw their main task as the service of the State. Educated in the civil law, they entered the royal service early and their bishop-rics were used by a penurious crown to support them as top civil servants. Rowland Lee, bishop of Coventry and Lichfield, for instance, spent most of his time putting down thieves on the Welsh border in his capacity as President of the Council in the Marches of Wales. Hanging was his main preoccupation, but he would turn his hand to most things and when the government ordered him to preach in support of the royal supremacy he agreed to try, 'though', as he said, 'I was never heretofore in pulpit'.

Cardinal Wolsey (1475–1530), unique in power and riches

Yet they were not all as philistine as Rowland Lee. Bishop Foxe, for 30 years or more Lord

Privy Seal, resigned his office in 1516 and 'utterly renounced the meddling in worldly matters, especially concerning the war... whereof.... I have no little remorse in my conscience'. Bishop Fisher, appointed to Rochester because even Henry VII felt obliged to promote to the bench at least one 'good and virtuous man', ended his life on the block for refusing to acknowledge Henry VIII as Supreme Head of the Church. The post-Reformation bishops were rather different. Certainly there were several time-servers among them, but there was also a substantial body of devout and learned theologians. Of the men appointed between 1485 and 1529 only Fisher could compare with Cranmer, Ridley, Jewel,

Archbishop Cranmer (1489–1556), a devout and scholarly churchman

and Hooker. The worst of the Elizabethan bishops were very unimpressive, but the best of them showed a devotion to the Church that their predecessors had mostly bestowed upon the state.

This growing devotion to the Church was matched by a decline in social status. The most influential Lancastrian bishops were often drawn from noble families: for instance, Archbishop Arundel was brother to an earl and Cardinal Beaufort was the illegitimate son of John of Gaunt. The episcopal bench of the early Tudor period was staffed by men of lesser birth, but its members had great political power and lived like feudal potentates, surrrounded by 'idle serving men and other moth-worms'. After the Reformation they were still able to muster a good following, but 'their wings were clipped' and they could no longer compete with the nobility for influence or prestige.

Clerical corruption

It is difficult to write fairly about the lower clergy of Tudor England. They were so often the object of attacks from religious reformers that the worst among them are too easily taken as typical. Many were more concerned with making a living than with preaching. Edward Kettle, rector of Semer in Suffolk, was reported to work 'in harvest time in binding of oats without any hat on his head, or doublet on his back, but only in his hose and shirt'. We get from this description a sharp image of the bucolic clergyman, little concerned with presenting a dignified figure to his parishioners.

Some of them were apparently rather worse than idle and bucolic. John Wainhouse, rector of Kirk-Smeaton, Yorkshire, was 'suspected to live incontinently with one Perkins, wife of the said town, and with certain other light women, comers and goers thither'. Not satisfied with this he also 'keepeth in his house one Frances Lancaster, a woman of evil conversation and an incontinent liver'. The Puritan *Register* of parish clergy, compiled under Elizabeth, makes shocking, though obviously partisan, revelations. 'Mr Goldring, parson of Langdon Hill, he was convicted of fornication, a drunkard. Mr Durden, parson of Mashbury, a careless man, a gamester, an alehouse haunter, a company keeper with drunkards, and he himself sometimes drunk.'

If there were gamblers and drunkards among the lower clergy there were also noble martyrs and good shepherds. One such was Vicar Walsh of St Thomas's, Exe Island, who led the south-western protest against the first prayer-book of Edward VI in 1549. Although he was ready to defy the government in defence of the old faith, he bravely prevented his fellow-rebels from setting fire to the city of Exeter. In reward he was hanged by the government forces in his mass-vestments, 'having a holy-water bucket, a sprinkle, a sacring bell, a pair of beads, and such other like popish trash hanged about him'. Another martyr, on the opposite side, was Rowland Taylor, incumbent of Hadley in Suffolk. Arrested in 1554, for continuing to use the Protestant liturgy, he was condemned to death and sent from London to his own parish for execution. So popular was he that his guards had to mask him so that he should not be recognised by the bystanders on his route. When he reached the common on which he was to be burned the people cried 'there goeth our good shepherd from us that so faithfully hath taught us'. Yet he turned aside all suggestion that he should conform, with the joke that he could not disappoint the worms in the churchyard, 'which should have had jolly feeding upon this carrion'. The dramatic lives and deaths of men like Walsh and Taylor should not obliterate the memory of the many parsons who devotedly ministered to their flocks without

The burning of Anne Askew and others at Smithfield, 1546

having to face martyrdom. For instance, there was Parson Atwell of St Ewe, in whose honour a ballad was written, called 'The poor sailor's praise of the parson of "Tue" in Cornwall, who feedeth the hungry, helpeth the sick, cureth the hurt etc.'; and there was the Reverend John Tomkis, for ten years preacher in Shrewsbury, called by one of his congregation the 'golden candlestick of doctrine'.

If others of the lower clergy fell far short of this standard in learning and devotion, the reason may partly be found in their social status. For many of them were said to be wretchedly poor. According to Archbishop Whitgift, half the livings in England were valued at less than £10 *per annum*. 'In many places', said Thomas Fuller, 'a small shiver of bread falls to the share of the minister, not enough for his necessary maintenance.' Such a reward hardly attracted the nobility and gentry, who 'wish their children anything, worldly lawyers, fraudulent merchants, killing physicians', rather than priests. In consequence, said the Church's critics, recruits for the ministry were too often from 'that base and starveling class, needy, vagabond, slaves of their own bellies, worthy to be sent back to the plough-tail, fitter for the pig-sty than the altar'.

But one should not follow the critics into exaggeration. Whitgift's estimate referred to official incomes, and in Tudor England these often omitted a good deal, or so one is bound to think if one considers the living standards of the clergy towards the end of the century. Some parsons lived in decent-sized houses which would have been too grand for all but the richest yeoman. The parsonage at Thorpe, Lincolnshire, for instance, had 16 rooms; and if that was unusually large, there were many that ran to a study for the parson and a room for the housemaid. The general rise in living standards between 1530 and 1600 seems very often to have been shared by the country parson. Many of them, by the later years of the century, were leaving sums of over £100 to their heirs—a good deal more than the average villager. Almost all of them had some books and they were fairly well off for clothes and plate. This picture of parsonical comfort matches the accounts, referred to earlier, of the prosperous yeoman. Both stood at the pinnacle of peasant

146

society and both were very far from poor. But essentially the living standards and the habits of the country parson were those of a rich peasant, since he depended for much of his comfort upon tithes given in kind or upon the products of that glebe land on which Parson Kettle toiled without hat or doublet. Thus his style of living, seeming humbler than it really was, presented few attractions to the sons of more pretentious classes.

The town parson was much less comfortably situated. While his tithes had very likely been commuted to a money-rent on extremely unfavourable terms, he could not so easily make up his income by working as a farmer upon his glebe. Unlike

Parsonage at Methwold, Norfolk

his country colleague, whose congregation, except for the squire, was much on a level with himself, the urban priest had to minister to merchants and tradesmen far richer than he. And nothing can be more irksome than that. Archbishop Laud said that 'the vicars in great market towns . . . are for the most part worst provided for', and Bishop Hooker wrote that 'a common artisan or tradesman of the City' was on a level with 'ordinary pastors of the Church'.

In such a situation some parsons found a relief in pluralism—holding more than one benefice at the same time. Bishop Hughes, saddled with the poor diocese of St Asaph, held 16 livings *in commendam*. Such were the men who 'heap up by hook or crook three or four fat livings [and] seldom preach at any of them, nor keep residence or hospitality'. Yet what could be done? Without pluralities, without non-resident

147

clergy, it would be impossible to attract learned men to the ministry or support scholarship at the universities. The dilemma was certainly painful, but one thing is clear: the beneficiaries of pluralism were the bishops and the upper clergy, for the really poor parson had not the necessary influence to ease his lot in this way.

The most obvious change in the condition of the clergy was the appearance of the parson's wife. Clerical marriage had first been allowed under Edward VI; in the reign of Mary married parsons had been given the alternative of abandoning their wives or their benefices; under her sister they were grudgingly allowed to reunite these blessings. Elizabeth made her own preference for a celibate clergy rudely plain when she said to Archbishop Parker's wife, '*Madam* I may not call you, and *Mistress* I am ashamed to call you, so I know not what to call you.' But she could not resist the Protestant demand for married parsons.

The effect of clerical marriage is difficult to gauge. Harrison thought that it was all for the best. Now that parsons had wives, 'their meat and drink is more orderly and frugally dressed, their furniture of household more convenient and better looked unto; and the poor oftener fed generally than heretofore they have been.' But the way of a parson's wife was rough, for people felt uncertain of her status, and consequently many women were reluctant to marry into the clergy. When children came, poverty was added to social slights. The Reverend Zachary Goddell wrote in 1615: 'my benefice is not worth above twenty marks [£13 6s. 8d.] by the year, my estate very poor, my children are ten'. He summed up the problems of a class.

In the bill for the suppression of the smaller monasteries the Crown proclaimed their 'manifest sin, vicious, carnal, and abominable living'. Was the accusation true? Certainly the monastic ideal had lost that drive which in the early Middle Ages filled the abbeys with devout men and endowed them with vast lands. No longer were they, as they had been in the tenth century, the only bastions of religion, charity, learning and civilisation. Other institutions had come to assist them and to rival them. But although there were, by the end of the Middle Ages, too few men of true religious vocation to fill them, the abbeys were still there, centres of vast estates, buildings large enough for many thousands. Either they had to remain unfilled or they must open their doors to men of less than the highest quality.

Such is the broad picture. But it would be absurd to say that there was no life in the monastic orders. In the last years of the fifteenth century monastic building entered a final and splendid phase. Leland described the work of Abbot Bere at Glastonbury: 'Richard Bere, abbot, built the new lodging by the great chamber called the

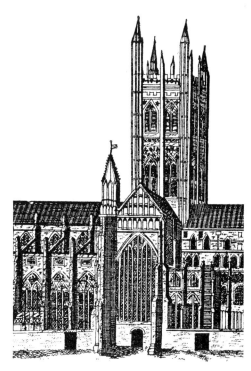

Bell Harry Tower, Canterbury, 1493–7, by John Wastell

king's lodging in the gallery. Bere builded the new lodgings for secular priests and clerks of our Lady.' He built part of Edgar's Chapel, shored up the east wall of the church when it began to 'cast out', made a 'rich altar of silver and gilt', built a chapel of our Lady of Loretto, a chapel of the sepulchre, and an almshouse. Nor did he build alone. Bell Harry tower at Canterbury, the Lady Chapel at Gloucester, the Prior's house at Much Wenlock, and the greater part of Bath Abbey, among a host of others, bear witness to the energy of his colleagues.

In most houses the numbers of the monks kept up fairly well. A few were almost empty but those were exceptions. By 1509 there were probably 12,000 monks in the country, more than there had been at any other time since the onset of the Black Death. Nor can the common charge be proved that a handful of monks was attended by a host of servants, for on average the numbers of servants and of monks were roughly equal.

149

Carthusian monks in prison

It is not easy to generalise about the condition of 12,000 monks in 550 monastic houses. A few were corrupt, a few excellent. Can one say more of the rest than that they were neither very good nor very bad? It seems fair to remark that no strong sense of vocation survived in English monasteries. When the attack came hardly any monks resisted and the vast majority were ready to go into the world; when, under Mary, there was the opportunity of revival not many took it. Perhaps one can compare the monks to many teachers and scholars in our schools and universities today: few have any overriding vocation for teaching or scholarship, most are there to make a decent professional living. It is bound to be thus and it is no disparagement to say so. Yet there are at least two critical differences between medieval monasteries and modern schools or universities. Most teachers are kept fully occupied and few of them live in celibate communities. The monks of the Tudor age, enclosed within the monastery walls, had no longer enough to do. The few with a real vocation could devote themselves to prayer, the few with a sense for learning could give their energies to scholarship. But with the invention of printing, the general growth of literacy, and the decline of manuscript illumination, many, who would in earlier centuries have been kept busy with the making of books, had now no function.

Inevitably gossip, dissension and grievances spread. Inefficient abbots were the target of bitter attacks. The abbot of Shrewsbury was said to provide no infirmary for the sick, to keep no accounts, to have sold a chalice, and to have allowed the roof over the high altar to fall down, so that 'the convent sit wet in the choir when it rains'. In such an atmosphere it was easy for Thomas Cromwell's visitors to pick up some useful scandals, succinctly reported by the witty Dr Layton, who told how the abbot of Bisham sold his household goods for 'white wine, sugar, borage leaves, and sack, whereof he sips nightly in his chamber till midnight', how the abbot of Battle was 'the veriest hayne [wretch], beetle, and buzzard, and the arrantest churl that ever I see'. To help the gossip on at least one of the visitors, Dr Thomas Legh, used inquisitorial methods:

Colchester Abbey church, just before the Dissolution

'wherever he comes he handles the fathers very roughly', complained one of his colleagues. In consequence of the spite and the rough handling, the visitors' final report had enough material to keep our Sunday newspapers in copy for years, and its tone finds an echo in gutter journalism—that peculiarly nasty inflection that springs from the moral indignation of men on the make. There is no need to repeat the catalogue of sexual failings. Some of the charges may well be true; others were contradicted by later investigations. At Garendon Abbey in Leicestershire Dr Layton and Dr Legh accused five monks of sodomy and reported that three wanted release from their vows. Later inspectors wrote of the monks that all were 'of good conversation, and God's service well maintained; all desire to continue in their religion or be assigned to some other house'. Although Garendon was rather surprisingly saved from suppression for the time being, this was not always so. At Buildwas Abbey in Shropshire the later inspectors found that the monks were 'all of good conversation and living by report, except the abbot, and God well and devoutly served by the prior and his brethren'. Yet the abbey was closed.

Even if one puts aside the evidence of Cromwell's visitors as highly exaggerated, the case against the monasteries is strong. Homes of vice and corruption they may not have been, but in many the old discipline was fading. The more dramatic and interesting sins were probably rare; small misdemeanours were common and unreformed. For instance, at Leicester in 1518 Abbot Pexall was found to have been generally slack, allowing a pack of hounds to be hunted by the monastic servants. He was suspended by Bishop Longland, but got back into office and within ten years had let discipline slip still further: now the canons themselves, as well as their servants, went hunting

A preserved monastic church: Tewkesbury, Gloucestershire

Romantic ruins: Fountains Abbey, Yorkshire

in the early morning, the hounds left their traces all over the monastery, and the abbot was accustomed to bring his fool with him into the choir. Worse perhaps than such jollity was the widespread custom of paying wages to the monks. These were not large—in Wales they ranged from 13*s*. 4*d*. to £2 13*s*. 4*d*. *per annum*—but they reveal that monastic life was becoming a profession rather than a dedication. If one cannot say that the moral tone of the monasteries was very bad, one certainly cannot say that it was very good. And if monks do not profess moral and religious excellence, what point lies in their survival?

As matters turned out, of course, they did not survive, although their suppression had no real connection with their moral failings. The Crown needed their money and their lands; and within five years of the visitation all the houses had gone, the monks and nuns sent into the world. To prevent the monks from coming back the commissioners were told to 'pull down to the ground all the walls of the churches, steeples, cloisters, fratries, dorters, chapter houses.' Some buildings were totally destroyed, men from the neighbourhood seizing what they could of stone and timber, others, like Fountains and Llanthony, became the romantic ruins of a later age, and a few survived, to become parish churches, like Tewkesbury, or cathedrals, like Gloucester and Chester.

The monks themselves did better. Abbots and priors were generously treated and several took high office in the Anglican Church: the abbot of Peterborough became bishop of the new see there, the abbot of Tewkesbury became bishop of Gloucester. Others had pensions which, considering the value of money at that time, were extraordinarily large: £300 a year to the ex-abbot of Bury St Edmunds, £100 to the ex-abbot of Chester, £40 to the ex-abbot of Whitby. The rank and file had to put up with something rather less lavish. At Shrewsbury, where the abbot was granted £80 a year, the prior got £10 a year, six monks got £6 apiece, five got £5 6s. 8d., two £5, and three only £1 6s. 8d. A yearly income of £5 was perhaps no more than a subsistence wage, but many of the monks were able to find benefices or part-time employment. For instance, 14 monks were turned out of Much Wenlock in 1540. One of them was already over 100 years old and another was a scholar at Oxford; the remaining 12 seem all to have added to their incomes by serving cures or chantries, mostly in the Wenlock area.

But this comfortable picture may conceal some awkward facts. Nuns were probably much worse off than monks, for where a monk could fend for himself and keep his independence, a nun could only return to live with her family, not always as a welcome guest. In a county like Shropshire where the monastic

Much Wenlock Priory, Shropshire, after the Dissolution

population was small, monks seem to have found employment, but in Yorkshire, with its large houses and few parishes, the market must have been much tighter. Here a monk might have to depend wholly upon his pension, which was not always paid promptly and was eroded in value by rising prices. He would consequently find himself in a situation familiar to many pensioners in our own day.

What was the impact of the Church upon laymen? And how did the changes of the Tudor epoch affect their religious life? In the sixteenth century, as in the Middle Ages, the Church was built into the whole structure of society in a way that is now hard to imagine. The parish vestry was an agent of secular government, electing constables, arranging for the upkeep of roads and providing for the relief of the poor. Christian festivals marked the progress of the farming year and, when 'holidays' really meant 'holy days', gave some respite from labour. The images and ornaments of his parish church were almost the only note of colour and beauty in the villager's life, the only objects of any value in which he could feel some proprietary sense. The impact of the Reformation was therefore felt in many compartments of life. To force home the truth that religion was a matter, not of externals, but of the inward spirit, reformers tore down screens, broke stained glass and destroyed images. An old inhabitant of Durham, looking back on his century from the year 1593, described the shrine carried in the Corpus Christi processions of his youth: it was 'all finely gilded, a goodly thing to behold, and on the height of the said shrine, was a four-squared box all of crystal, wherein was enclosed the holy sacrament of the altar'. In 1548 one of the royal commissioners, 'appointed to deface all such ornaments', 'did tread upon it with his feet and did break it all in pieces'. Festivals and celebrations were also attacked by the reformers. According to Harrison there had been 95 feast days and 30 saints' eves in papal times. These were reduced, he says, to 27, 'and with them the superfluous number of idle wakes, guilds, fraternities, church-ales, . . . with the heathenish rioting at brideales, are well diminished and laid aside.' In towns the Tudor monarchs, afraid of dissension, helped to suppress the religious plays and pageants of the guilds, while in Wales the bards and minstrels were sharply cut down in number.

It is impossible to assess, but fatal to ignore, the change wrought in the quality of life by the disappearance of festivals, plays, pageants, and things of beauty. Yet all was not changed at once. At least until 1570, and perhaps thereafter, there was in much of England a deep nostalgia for the traditional ways. When the northern earls rebelled in 1569, holy-water vats were built and old practices revived. In North Wales pilgrimages continued under the leadership of the bards, 'who, at the direction of some old gentlewoman, do ordinarily give the summons of the time certain for such meetings'; and the Bishop of Bangor commented on his people that 'ignorance continueth many in the dregs of superstition'. Nor was it only in Wales that superstition flourished. Astrology and prophecy were as popular as ever, and strange happenings were quickly seized upon as omens. When a pig was born with 'a head much like unto a dolphin's head', it was thought that God had sent it as a message and that 'these strange monstrous sights do premonstrate unto us that His heavy indignation will shortly come upon us for our monstrous living'.

The lower orders of society remained largely passive in all the process of change, clinging to what they could of the old ways, but slowly losing much of their traditional life. At the upper end of society laymen played a more active role in spiritual affairs and began to wield a greater influence over the Church than ever before. With the dissolution of the monasteries, they struck a severe blow against the morale and prestige of the clerical estate, for it was obvious to everyone thereafter that lands and buildings intended for divine purposes and spiritual men could be seized by the laity for its own benefit. More particularly, landowners took over some of the ecclesiastical rights once held by monastic houses. The long-established power of laymen to appoint clergy to benefices was now greatly extended, so that they were able to mould the spiritual life of a parish: 'if the patron be precise, so must his chaplain be; if he be papistical, his clerk must be so, or else be turned out.' Their rights even stretched beyond such influence into church revenues. For parochial tithes had often been credited, or impropriated, to monastic houses and could now be purchased by laymen. When money or goods intended for a spiritual purpose—the maintenance of the priesthood—went to supplement the rent-rolls of the gentry, a protest was inevitable, and Milton's attack upon 'the ignoble hucksterage of piddling tithes' was only one of many.

But this lay influence should not be interpreted as the advance of a secular spirit. For in many ways religion was enabled by the development of the printing-press and the circulation of books in English to penetrate men's lives more deeply than it had done for generations. William Tyndale's translation of the Bible in the 1520s was the first of a long series, and, although Tyndale's own achievement was regarded as heretical, Thomas Cromwell later encouraged the production of the Great Bible on behalf of the Crown. The title-page of that work shows very well the relationship of Church and State, with Henry VIII enthroned in glory, handing the text to his bishops while the crowd shouts *vivat rex*. But however much the Great Bible may have expounded the supremacy of the King, it also brought to the laity an intelligible version of the scriptures, and with the appearance of the lighter and more easily handled Geneva Bible in

Henry VIII's Great Bible of 1539

of thefe latter and perillous dayes,
touching matters of the Church, wherein
ar comprehended and defcribed the great perfecu-
tions & horrible troubles, that have bene wrought
and practifed by the Romifhe Prelates, fpecial-
lye in this Realme of England and Scot-
lande, from the yeare of our Lorde a
thoufande, unto the tyme
nowe prefent.

Gathered and collected according to the
true copies & wrytinges certificatorie as wel
of the parties them felues that fuffered, as
alfo out of the Bifhops Regifters,
which wer the doers thereof,
by Iohn Foxe.

¶ Imprinted at London by Iohn Day,
dwellyng over Alderfgate.

Cum priuilegio Regie Maieftatis.

Title-page of Foxe's ' Book of Martyrs', 1563

1557, the Word of God was available for all who could read.

Standing beside the Bible as the foundation of English piety was John Foxe's *Actes and Monuments of these latter and perillous Dayes*, better known as *The Book of Martyrs*. Its title-page shows its purpose: on the left-hand side are the risen saints, the English protestant martyrs, and a congregation listening to the Word of God; on the right are the emissaries of the Catholic Church being cast out of heaven by demons. The book was a best-seller in its own day and long after. It went into five editions in the reign of Elizabeth, was placed in all cathedrals, bishops' palaces, city orphanages, and halls of city companies, and was taken by Francis Drake on his journey round the world. It was no bloodthirsty account of atrocities, but an eloquent plea that 'because God hath so placed us Englishmen here in one commonwealth, also in one church, as in one ship together, let us not mangle or divide the ship'. Together with the English Bible it gave the nation a sense of divine mission that ran very deep.

This sense had its active and practical expression in charitable giving. In the Middle Ages men gave their money in alms to the beggars at their gates or to the Church. Monasteries, churches, and chantries were the great objects of charity. But

158

even in the early years of the sixteenth century dissatisfaction with the clergy was turning some men away from such giving: London schools, as we have seen, were put under lay rather than clerical control. Then, at the breach with Rome, donations to the Church fell sharply and for a time the money that once went to spiritual ends stayed in the pockets of its owners. 'Men', said the preacher Thomas Becon, '. . . are the "lovers of themselves", and not of the poor . . .. They heap to themselves, they provide nothing for the poor.' With the social crisis of mid-century to spur them on, Becon, Latimer and other preachers drove their congregations into more generous giving. 'Why', asked one of them, 'do we so gape for riches, why do we dedicate all our labour to unjust mammon?' 'Christianity', said another, 'is not an idle profession, but a busy practice, always occupied in doing good.' Their words took effect. From about 1550 the volume of charity began to surge upwards until by 1620 it had, in terms of real income, regained the highest level of pre-Reformation days. More important than the volume of charity was the change in its direction. In place of largely casual giving men put their bequests into charitable trusts, which could form a permanent foundation for their objective; and they turned their charity away from the Church towards education and the rehabilitation of the poor. But their motives were far from being entirely secular; for their actions were directed by a faith concerned with 'the better relief of the poor, the maintenance of learning, and the setting forth of God's Word'.

Further Reading

H. Maynard Smith, *Pre-Reformation England*, 1938
M. C. Knowles, *The Religious Orders in England: Vol. III, The Tudor Age*, 1959
Glanmor Williams, *The Welsh Church from Conquest to Reformation*, 1962
A. Tindal Hart, *The Country Clergy in Elizabethan and Stuart Times*, 1958
Christopher Hill, *The Economic Problems of the Church*, 1956
W. K. Jordan, *Philanthropy in England 1480-1660*, 1959

VIII

Change and Rebellion

The changes that took place in Tudor England seem slow and unremarkable beside the huge advances in technology, the terrifying elaboration of weapons, and the social transformations of this century. But we live in an age when change seems as natural as the movement of the seasons, when historians have accustomed us to the mutations of past societies, when politicians daily exhort us to go forward, and when few people, even of the most conservative instincts, would consent to being called 'reactionary'. In the sixteenth century very few people would have willingly been called anything else.

For Englishmen of that time were firmly rooted in the belief that change was wrong and they saw human society as a part of that great chain of being which stretched from the Almighty to the lowest animals: 'God', said Henry VII's notorious minister, Edmund Dudley, 'God hath set an order by grace between Himself and angel, and between angel and angel; and by reason between the angel and man, and between man and man, man and beast; . . . which order from the highest point to the lowest God willeth us firmly to keep.' Within this hierarchy each man had his place and his vocation: in the words of John Hales, opponent of enclosure and defender of the peasantry, it has 'pleased God . . . to ordain in the commonwealth divers degrees of people; some to be governors, rulers and defenders of it . . . and others to be his victuallers and purveyors of things necessary for the use and sustenance of man.' Any alteration to this fixed and determined order seemed shocking.

So the decline of communities and the impoverishment of their inhabitants were, quite naturally, alarming. 'Who', said the humanist Thomas Starkey, 'can be so blind or obstinate to deny the great decay, faults, and misorders here of our commonwealth, either when he looketh upon our cities, castles, and towns of late days ruinate and fallen down . . . or when he looketh upon the ground, so rude and so waste?' Men had been turned out of their homes, so that where there were 'eight, ten, twelve, yea sixteen households and more, is now but a sheep-house and two or three shepherds'. Corn-growing, 'the very paunch of the commonwealth', had been put down in favour of sheep, so that bread prices were too high for poor men to live: 'it was never merry with poor craftsmen since gentlemen became graziers . . . Now we are scant able to live without debt.' The rich, who had done well out of the miseries of the poor, were too niggardly to help their neighbours: 'in London', preached Latimer, 'their brother shall die in the street for cold, he shall lie sick at the door between stock and stock. . . . Charity is waxen cold.'

Riches shocked as much as poverty, for decay went side by side with the prosperity of new classes and an unprecedented taste for luxury. Lawyers were thriving on the fashion for litigation, actors and impresarios on the demand for spectacle and display. Craftsmen, instead of being put to traditional and useful tasks, were now ill occupied 'in making and procuring things for the vain pastime and pleasure of others', in 'guarding and jagging of men's apparel', in procuring 'new kinds of meats and drinks', in devising 'new-fangled things concerning the vain pleasure only of the

The miser and the prodigal: a satire

Fools playing cards: a satire on gambling and dissipation

body'. Noblemen had too many idle retainers to serve them—'Look', said Starkey, 'what an idle rout our noblemen keep and nourish in their houses!' The riches of the nation were drained off to pay for luxury imports—'glasses, as well looking as drinking, . . . glass windows, dials, tables, cards, balls, puppets, penhorns, inkhorns, tooth-picks, gloves'—while Englishmen no longer wanted the goods of their own country.

When society was so far out of joint men looked for a scapegoat. Clergy-baiting, a sport at least as old as Wyclif and the Lollards, gained new vigour from a growing sense of desperation at the changing order. To end the abuses, said the ex-friar, Henry Brinkelow, 'ye must first down with all your vain chantries, all your proud colleges of canons and specially your forked wolves, the bishops', for here was the source of idleness: 'look to our bishops and prelates of the realm . . . look, furthermore, to priests, monks, friars, and canons, with all their "adherenty" and idle train, and you shall find also among them no small number idle and unprofitable.' But the clergy were not the only target. Landlords, by raising their rents, were thought to be a canker in the realm. 'Consider you', said Brinkelow, 'what a wickedness is commonly used thorough the realm unpunished, in the inordinate enhauncing of rents and taking of unreasonable fines.' All the trouble grew 'thorough the great dropsy and the insatiable desire of riches of rich men'. They were caterpillars of the commonwealth, covetous persons, extortioners, insatiable cormorants, and greedy gulls. Merchants and usurers were also blamed, for they brought in unnecessary luxuries, drove up the price of cloth, and demanded huge rates of interest upon loans. Even the Reverend William

162

Harrison, generally a cool and uncensorious writer, worked up a rage against the merchants: 'it is to be wished,' he remarked, 'that the huge heap of them were somewhat restrained.'

Most men agreed that the trouble sprang from moral corruption, greed and desire. One or two writers saw that men would always want money. 'Can we devise that all covetousness may be taken from men? No, no more than we can make men to be without ire, without gladness, without fear, and without all affections.' To men who thought like this the remedy was to take away the temptation, and so to arrange the economy that greed did the minimum of harm. But so modern an outlook was rare and most men sought religious remedies for a moral disease. 'We remain also, and continue still, in a perpetual bondage and spiritual captivity.' Men must seek the glory of God, and 'whereas ye have sought every man his own private or particular wealth, now seek your neighbours' wealth as your own'.

Most famous of all these exhortations was the *Utopia* of Sir Thomas More, scholar, ascetic, lawyer, statesman, and martyr— 'the singular ornament' of his age. More looked first at the lamentable disorders of England. Here the gentry 'poll and shave to the quick' their tenants in order that they may 'not only live in idleness themselves, but also carry about with them at their tails a great flock or train of idle and loitering serving men'. The wool growers 'leave no ground for tillage, they enclose all into pastures; they throw down houses; they pluck down towns and leave nothing standing, but only the church to be made a sheephouse.' Husbandmen and labourers were thrown off the land with no choice but to beg or steal. If they begged they were imprisoned as vagabonds; if they

Sir Thomas More (1478–1535), Lord Chancellor, writer and martyr

163

From Sir Thomas More's 'Utopia', 1518

stole they were hanged. Contrast this with the state of Utopia! Its people had not even the teaching of Christ to help them, yet every man, except for a few chosen scholars, worked with his hands and produced enough to satisfy the needs of all. Here property was held in common and no man felt the urge to enrich himself at the expense of his neighbour. How did they avoid the calamities of England? They were happy because they were free from the 'one only beast, the princess and mother of all mischief, pride', from which all greed, oppression, luxury and poverty grew. For men were not content with comforts and riches unless they could lord it over others who were less fortunate. Pride would never be satisfied 'if there were no wretches left over whom she might, like a scornful lady, rule and triumph, over whose miseries her felicities might shine, whose poverty she might vex, torment and increase by gorgeously setting forth her riches'. If pride could be plucked out all would be well.

The protests quoted came from educated men: from Sir Thomas More, Lord Chancellor; from Thomas Starkey, humanist; from Henry Brinkelow, ex-Franciscan and citizen of London; from John Hales, civil servant and member of parliament; from Hugh Latimer, bishop and preacher. But they were not alone in their protests, for popular voices also were raised in anger. Ballads spoke on behalf of the oppressed:

164

Alas, alas it is great pity
That rich men be so blind
Which for their great pride and fulsome fare,
They pluck and pull their neighbours bare.

and

. . . From pillar to post,
The poor man he was toss'd,
I mean the labouring man,
I mean the husband man,
I mean the plough man,
I mean the handicraft man,
I mean the victualling man,
And also the good yeoman,
That sometime in this realm,
Had plenty of 'key' and cream,
Butter, eggs and cheese,
Honey, wax and bees,
But now alack, alack,
All these men go to wrack.

Peasants were not content with rhymes; in county after county they took matters into their own hands. On the Somerset lands of Sir John Rodney they pulled down and burned enclosure fencing. When Sir John went to stop them 'John Webb with a pitchfork struck two times at the said Sir John, intending to have slain him'. Luckily for Sir John another peasant, more cautious, intervened, saying 'let us not slay him, for he is our master'. At that Sir John prudently retreated and left them to their burning. When a Montgomeryshire landlord enclosed a piece of common land the angry commoners, in women's clothes, occupied the land, declared themselves to be 'lords and rulers here' and cut down several oak trees. When the justices of the peace intervened, the rioters, saying that they would chop up the trees 'small as herbs to the pot', ploughed up the common and protested that before giving up the lands they would 'die upon them'.

These were minor incidents, typical of the countless riots that took place in the middle of the sixteenth century, More dramatic and more serious were the rebellions. In October 1536 a rising in Lincolnshire spread quickly north to Yorkshire and the border country, when 30,000 Pilgrims of Grace under the leadership of Robert Aske demanded that the dissolved monasteries be restored and that many other grievances be remedied. Henry VIII's skill in playing for time and the rebels' trust in his worthless promises enabled the Crown to regain control. Thirteen years later the government of the young Edward VI was faced with a double rising. About 6,000 men of Devon and Cornwall protested against the new Protestant prayer-book and besieged Exeter. In the following month Robert Ket and 15,000 men threw down enclosures in Norfolk, encamped on Mousehold Heath outside Norwich, and demanded that the government prevent landlords from encroaching on the common pastures. Both groups of rebels stayed on their home ground rather than advance upon the capital, and the government was in consequence able to put them down easily enough by choosing its moment.

The two rebellions that took place after 1550 differed from

Norwich, the second city in the country and

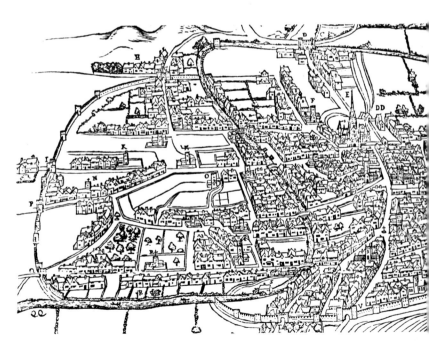

these earlier movements in being initiated by landowners rather than by peasants. In 1554 a large group of noblemen, alarmed at the prospect of Queen Mary's marriage to the foreign prince, Philip of Castile, plotted risings in Kent, the Midlands, the Welsh Marches, and the South-West. When their plans leaked out, they were forced to move too soon and only one of the leaders, the Kentish Sir Thomas Wyatt, got his rebellion

Sir Thomas Wyatt (1521–54)

under way. Yet this was dangerous enough, for the rebels were able to occupy Southwark and to reach the walls of the City itself before Mary's courage and the loyalty of the citizens brought their defeat. In 1568 the flight of Mary Queen of Scots to England encouraged some of the discontented nobility to plan her marriage to the leading English aristocrat, the duke of Norfolk. When in 1569 Elizabeth discovered the plan, forbade the marriage and imprisoned the duke, two of his allies, the

the scene of Robert Ket's rebellion in 1549

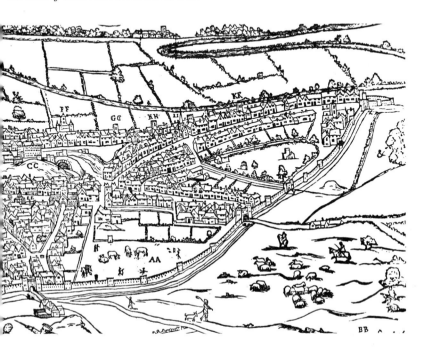

northern earls of Northumberland and Westmorland, blundered into rebellion. They and their retainers marched south through Yorkshire, trying to rescue Mary. But when this failed, they turned back to the border and found their followers gradually dwindling in numbers until flight was the only possible course. Many of the fears and tensions of Tudor society are revealed by these rebellions. At Louth in Lincolnshire, where the Pilgrimage of Grace began, the townspeople were proud of their parish church with its fine new steeple and feared that its ornaments would be confiscated by the king. As the Michaelmas procession wound through the town, one Thomas Foster said to his neighbour: 'go we to follow the crosses, for and if they be taken from us we be like to follow them no more'. This fear for the local church sparked off the great movement of protest that later found its main grievance in the royal destruction of the monasteries. Similar fears for their ornaments and their accustomed ceremonies drove the men of Devon and Cornwall into rebellion against the Edwardian liturgy, which they dismissed as a 'Christmas game'.

Fear of agrarian change was as potent as fear of religious reformation. The followers of Robert Ket in 1549 wanted to preserve the commons from the landlords, keep down rents, and ensure that 'all bond men may be made free, for God made all free with his precious blood-shedding'. The Cumberland peasants in 1536 rose less from anger at the dissolution of the monasteries than in protest against their landlords. They refused to pay rent, pulled down enclosures, and assembled under the leadership of a man who called himself Captain Poverty. Yet in 1536 religious and economic grievances were indistinguishably mixed: Yorkshiremen disliked the dissolution because they feared that it would drain money away to the south; borderers, mainly concerned though they were with enclosure, protested also against the abolition of holidays and festivals.

Noblemen, gentry and peasants alike strongly resented interference by the central government in local affairs. More than anything else the northern earls in 1569 disliked the Queen's appointment of southerners to the great border commands and the favour that she showed to the upstart William

Cecil. In the Pilgrimage of Grace the hatred of northcountry-men was focused upon Thomas Cromwell, who was set up as the scapegoat for all their discontents. 'Cromwell', said the rebel Lord Darcy, 'it is thou that art the very original and chief causer of all this rebellion and mischief.' His words show the potent hatred of the aristocrat for the 'new man' and of the regional nobility for the central administration.

The penalty of failure: the execution of Edmond Geninges, 1591

Fears were easily fed upon rumour. A story that Spanish troops had landed on the south coast brought recruits to Sir Thomas Wyatt in 1554. Ket's rebellion was set off in 1549 by reports that enclosures had been thrown down in Kent. Most remarkable of all was the web of rumour that spread through the north in 1536: it was said that the king intended to seize all Church jewels, that no church should be allowed to stand within five miles of another, that all men would have to hand their gold over to the exchequer, and that no man should eat white bread or capons without paying a fine. These stories were of course fantastic: but their ready reception shows how suspicious and anxiety-ridden provincial society had become.

But however revealing the rebellions may be as the clinical symptoms of social illness, we have to remember that they failed. Their support was drawn from rural areas—from backwoods gentry and peasants—and they lacked that urban backing which was so important to the parliamentary rebels of the seventeenth century. The regional isolation of Tudor England hampered them all: they were Kentish, Cornish, or northern, but never national, rebellions. Nor did the rebels show that determination and ferocity which is necessary for success. When Ket's rebels were getting out of hand the vicar of St Martin's, Norwich, and some of his choristers sang them a *Te Deum*, 'by the sweetness of which song, they being ravished (for they were unwonted to music), their cruel and raging minds (bewitched with these unaccustomed delights) by little and little were appeased'. True revolutionaries would hardly be calmed by a *Te Deum*.

Above all, the great majority of gentry and magnates stayed loyal to the government. True, the Percies supported rebellion in 1536 and 1569, while several noblemen showed their hostility to the government in 1554. True, some of the local gentry put up a poor showing against the rebels: one official said that he had never seen 'such a sight of asses' as the Lincolnshire J.P.s in 1536. But by and large the landed classes kept aloof from rebellion and helped to crush it. The reason, which I hope has been demonstrated in this book, is that they were comfortable and prosperous under Tudor rule. In this situation the grievances of the less fortunate had little hope of finding redress.

Further Reading

Thomas More, *Utopia*, Latin edn. 1516; English translation by Ralph Robinson, 1551
J. Huizinga, *The Waning of the Middle Ages*, 1924
R. H. Tawney, *Religion and the Rise of Capitalism*, 1926
—— ——, *The Agrarian Problem in the Sixteenth Century*, 1912
Helen C. White, *Social Criticism in Popular Religious Literature of the Sixteenth Century*, 1944
S. T. Bindoff, *Ket's Rebellion*, 1949

Index

The numerals in **heavy type** refer to the pages on which illustrations appear

171